Praise for *Thesis and Conviction*

For years as a close family friend, I've had the privilege of watching Steve Ankerstar live the very principles he writes about in this book: the disciplined crafting of a clear, evidence-based thesis and the quiet, unyielding conviction to see it through—no matter the challenge. From his days as a stealth fighter pilot, through building Ankerstar Wealth into a respected, forward-thinking firm, to raising a family with deep purpose and integrity, Steve has consistently shown how thoughtful analysis paired with resolute commitment creates not just financial success, but a life of real meaning and impact. I've seen these qualities in action time and again, and they shine through every page here. This isn't theory for Steve—it's who he is. A heartfelt, inspiring read that reflects the man I've known and admired for so long.

Dr. Judy Staveley
CEO & Founder, *The Platform Magazine*

Steve Ankerstar and Mike Younkman embody the essence of what this book teaches: crafting a sharp, evidence-based thesis and backing it with relentless conviction to create extraordinary outcomes. When MedCana needed strategic capital to fuel our growth in pharmaceutical-grade cannabis—building premium extracts, expanding global supply chains, and navigating a complex, emerging industry—they stepped in with precisely that mindset. Their disciplined analysis of our vision, combined with unwavering commitment through market volatility and regulatory hurdles, helped us secure the funding to accelerate our mission. Steve and Mike don't just advise on investments; they live the principles of thoughtful conviction that turn high-potential ideas into real-world success. This book is a masterclass in applying those same tools to build wealth, lead businesses, and seize transformative opportunities—exactly what they've done for us and countless others.

Gabriel Diaz
CEO, MedCana

Before working with Mike and the Ankerstar Wealth team, I had real concerns about my retirement planning and portfolio performance. I had known Mike for years and long admired his work ethic, creative thinking, and ability to execute with excellence. When he joined Ankerstar Wealth, I did not hesitate to move my wealth planning to the firm.

Since then, my confidence has only grown. I am so pleased with how my portfolio is being managed that I am now working with the team to pass assets on to my children. Ankerstar Wealth is consistently responsive and communicative and—most important—has delivered strong returns at fair, transparent fees.

I have tremendous respect for this team and am excited to see them release a book to share their approach with a broader audience.

Ben Colman
Former CEO of Vizium360 and Women's Health New York

Steve Ankerstar and Mike Younkman bring a powerful, real-world fusion of rigorous thesis and unshakeable conviction to every aspect of wealth management—not just in their high-conviction portfolios, but in how they've built and scaled Ankerstar Wealth into a forward-thinking, client-first RIA. As the outsourced CTO partner for their firm through AdvizorStack, I've witnessed firsthand the disciplined strategic thinking and bold execution that define their approach: from evaluating cutting-edge fintech integrations to committing to innovative, theme-driven strategies that deliver lasting value in volatile markets. This book captures that same rare combination—thoughtful analysis paired with resolute follow-through—that empowers advisors and investors alike to navigate complexity with confidence. Steve and Mike don't just preach these principles; they live them, and the results speak for themselves. A compelling, actionable read for anyone serious about superior outcomes in investing and independent advisory.

Nico DeMaio
President & Founder, AdvizorStack

In a beta-dominated world, Steve Ankerstar and Mike Younkman make a compelling case for why strong thesis and unrelenting conviction are the true drivers of alpha. At Cyber Hornet ETFs, we've built our strategy around that same forward-looking conviction—bridging the proven strength of the S&P 500 with the transformative power of Bitcoin and digital assets to give investors and advisors balanced, innovative exposure to the future of wealth.

Todd Johnson
Co-Founder, CYBER HORNET ETFs

I had the pleasure of meeting the Ankerstar team in Miami in early 2025. It was immediately clear that Mike and Steve genuinely cared about retail investors. They shared Autopilot's vision of making great portfolio management accessible to anyone through simple interfaces and automated trading. Ankerstar quickly saw the opportunity and partnered with Autopilot—creator of the famous Pelosi Tracker—to bring their models to market, ranging from the Bitcoin Alpha portfolio to Quantum Xtreme and the EGO-10.

Ankerstar Wealth is exactly the type of manager Autopilot was built to empower. They have strong views on where markets are going, and they build real structure around those views. Every model comes with clear risk parameters, and they've thought carefully about how these portfolios actually behave in a real client account. That kind of discipline is rarer than it sounds in this space. They're also among the first RIAs to offer their models through a simple subscription, putting them on the cutting edge of scalable innovation.

Aaron Langley
Co-Founder of Autopilot

What sets Ankerstar apart from other advisors is their willingness to learn and expand into new areas. Whether it is crypto or a new strategy, they seek to evolve in order to serve their clients well. They are not afraid to take risks by using products others avoid because they are not large enough or do not trade frequently enough. This is what sets Steve, Mike, and the rest of the team apart.

Edward Rosenberg

ETF Industry Leader

President, The Platform Magazine Foundation

Author, Educator, and Advocate in STEM, Biotechnology, and Wellness

THESIS
AND
CONVICTION

INVESTING FOR ALPHA
IN A BETA WORLD

STEVEN E. ANKERSTAR, CFP®, MBA
MICHAEL P. YOUNKMAN, MBA

STORY CHORUS

Thesis and Conviction

ISBN: 978-1-955362-35-1

Published by Story Chorus (www.storychorus.com)

Dedication

This book is dedicated to **Bradley Ankerstar,** whose life was a powerful demonstration of thesis and conviction. He held a clear, principled thesis about what matters most—integrity in leadership, humility in service, and selfless love for family—and backed it with the kind of quiet, unshakable conviction that carried him through every season. His example remains the North Star for our family, our firm, and the ideas expressed here. Though he is no longer physically present, his legacy endures in the steady application of those same principles that guide our lives and this work.

Table of Contents

Introduction:

The $8 Million Surprise

I (Steve) remember the day clearly. A client and I met at the University of Texas tennis complex. He had sent me all his paperwork in advance. Bank statements. Investment accounts. Property records. Everything was in a stack of folders that must have weighed five pounds. When we sat down at a table outside, he was nervous. His wife was with him, and they both looked a little embarrassed.

"We've got a bunch of stuff," he said. "But we don't really have our arms around everything we have."

I had spent a few hours going through all their documents. I added everything up. I checked my math twice. Then I checked it a third time because I couldn't believe what I was seeing.

"So," I said. "What do you think you're worth?"

He looked at his wife. She shrugged.

"Right around $4 million," he said. "Maybe a little less."

I turned my laptop around so they could see the screen. The financial planning software showed all their accounts, everything organized and totaled.

"You're worth $8 million," I said.

His jaw dropped. His wife grabbed his arm. They both stared at the screen like I had just shown them a winning lottery ticket.

"Are you serious?" he asked.

I walked them through every line item. The retirement accounts they had forgotten about, their rental properties, the investments they had scattered across different firms—it was all there. It was all there. They just had never put it all together in one place.

That meeting was years ago, and that client is now one of our biggest advocates. He tells everyone the same story: "I had no idea how wealthy I was until I sat down with Steve. You have to work with these guys."

Here's the funny part: He still works eighty hours a week. Even though he knows he never has to work another day in his life, nothing changed because he loves what he does. But at least now he knows.

The Other Side of the Story

I (Mike) wish every story ended that way, but most don't. Often, I sit across from someone who thinks they're on track for retirement. They've been saving for twenty years and feel good about their position. Then we run the numbers. The math doesn't work.

They think they can retire at sixty-five years old. But with what they've saved and how much they're spending, they'd run out of money at seventy-five. And they might live to ninety-five; that's a problem.

Or I meet someone who's fifty-five years old, has fifty thousand dollars saved, and wants to retire by sixty-seven. The calculator doesn't lie. Social Security will cover some of what they need to survive, but not nearly enough.

These conversations are hard. Nobody wants to hear they're off track. But it's better to know now than to discover it at sixty-seven when it's too late to fix. The unknown is stressful. At least with a clear picture, you can plan, make changes, and adjust.

We like to say we're in the business of helping people know where they truly are—not where they hope they are, not where they assume they are, but where they actually are—because you can't plan for the future if you don't understand the present.

Who We Are

We've been friends since high school. We're from the same small town in Ohio, took the same math classes, and always had the same competitive drive that pushed us to be better. I (Steve) got a thirty-four on the math portion of the ACT. I was pretty proud of that. I missed one question out of the whole test. The school made a big deal about it. Teachers were congratulating me. I felt like a genius. Then Mike took the test and got a thirty-six, a perfect score.

I was so mad that I retook the test. I studied harder, determined to tie him.

And wouldn't you know it, I got another thirty-four. So thirty years later, I hired Mike!

We laugh about it now. But it shows you who we are. We're competitive. We push each other. We don't settle for good enough. And we've been doing this since we were teenagers.

We both went into the military. I joined the Air Force and became a fighter pilot. I flew in combat. I learned about risk management the hard way. When you're flying a jet that costs $40 million, and one mistake could kill you, you learn to assess risk carefully and quickly.

I (Mike) joined the Ohio Army National Guard as a combat engineer. We built bridges, cleared floods, and worked as a team to solve complex problems. I learned that different people bring different skills. The best results come when everyone works together.

After the military, our paths split for a while. Steve stayed in the Air Force for twenty years while I went into computer science and business consulting. But we stayed friends. We stayed competitive. And we both stayed interested in investing.

I (Steve) started studying investing in eighth grade. My math teacher, who also sold insurance, showed me a time-value-of-money chart. From the moment I saw the power of compound interest, I was hooked. So, I did what any normal eighth-grader would do: I asked for a subscription to *The Wall Street Journal* for my birthday. I couldn't understand most of it at first, but I kept reading, even though I didn't have anyone to talk to about what I was trying to learn. There weren't a lot of people in our small town who talked about the stock market. But along the way, I did get some unexpected career advice.

Our small town had an interesting claim to fame: Neil Armstrong lived there. Yes, that Neil Armstrong—the first man on the moon. After returning from space, he wanted a quiet life away from the spotlight and he chose the little hamlet of Lebanon, Ohio.

You'd see him around town. He came to all our high school basketball games, sat by himself in the stands, just watched. Everyone in town knew who he was, but people respected his privacy and tried not to bother him. He was just part of the community.

My dad was a teacher and a coach at the high school. He knew Neil from being around the school so much. They weren't close friends, but they were friendly.

One day, my dad and I went to play golf at our local course. It was nothing fancy, just a small course where everyone in town played. That day, the clubhouse paired us up with someone else, Neil Armstrong.

I didn't say much at first. I was just a kid, and he was a legend. What do you say to someone who walked on the moon? However, Neil was friendly enough. As we played, he started asking me questions. At one of the holes, he asked what I wanted to study in college.

"Mathematics," I said.

He shook his head. "You don't want to do that."

I stared at him blankly, in shock. I had no idea what to say in reply, as my plans were just dashed against the rocks of an astronaut's opinion.

As if reading my mind, he explained, "They'll lock you in a basement without windows. Be an engineer instead. Then you can actually apply math to real things."

Fast forward to college, and I became an engineer. But I kept investing my money on the side.

I (Mike) came to investing differently. I spent my twenties making money and spending it as fast as it came in. I thought that was what life was about: Build the biggest number you can, have fun, repeat.

Then, in my early thirties, I became a Christian and *everything* changed. I realized there was more to life than just accumulating money. There was purpose, meaning, and stewardship beyond a big bank account. So I went back to school and got a master's degree in Christian leadership. I started leading small groups at church and learned that the skills I used in business could help people in other areas of life—everything connected in a new and exhilarating way.

How We Built Ankerstar Wealth

I (Steve) started Ankerstar Wealth after retiring from the Air Force. I knew I didn't want to fly for the airlines, as that sounded boring. I wanted to do what I'd dreamed of since eighth grade: help people invest. But I wanted to do it differently. I didn't want to work for a big firm where they tell you exactly what to say and what to sell. I wanted to build something from scratch something that really helped people.

I hired my first employee, Candice, who had been teaching kindergarten. She was a family friend, so my wife and I had known her for years. I'd watch her talk about her job at family gatherings. At first, she loved it, lighting up every time she talked about teaching.

But over time, something changed. She started saying things like, "I can't do this forever." Kindergarten is exhausting. You're on your feet all day. You're managing twenty-five little kids who all need something different. It wears you down.

I started thinking: She would be perfect for what I'm building. She's organized. She's patient. She knows how to explain complicated things simply. That's exactly the kind of person I need.

But I couldn't just offer her a job out of nowhere. I needed the right moment. I needed her to be ready for a change.

So I waited. I kept the idea in the back of my mind. And I kept listening.

One day, I called her. "Weird idea," I said. "Can I come over some evening and talk to you and your husband about something?"

She said yes. So I went over to their house, sat at their kitchen table, and laid it all out. "I've actually been thinking about this for a year," I told them. "This is the first time I'm saying it out loud, but I think you'd be perfect for my company."

She thought about it, talked it over with her husband, and said yes. That was years ago. She's still with us today as our operations manager, running the behind-the-scenes of everything we do. Hiring her was one of the best decisions I've ever made.

Then I hired more people. I wanted people who understood service—a retired Air Force colonel who loved investing, then another former teacher. Each person was intentional. I wanted people who understood service. And today, the firm is split evenly between former teachers and military members. In short, Ankerstar is filled with people who care more about helping than selling.

When the opportunity to hire Mike came up, I jumped on it. He had been a client and was a lifelong friend, so I knew how smart he was and how hard he worked. I also knew we thought about investing the same way, even while we brought different perspectives.

I (Mike) was working at a tech startup when everything fell apart. The company went bankrupt and on a Friday afternoon, my boss called and said, "This is the call you never wanted. Get your team together. At 5 p.m., all systems shut down."

Two hours' notice. No severance. No insurance. Nothing. I called Steve to let him know I was hitting the job market. I wasn't asking for a job; I was giving him a heads-up as a friend and as a client.

The next day, he called back and said, "I'd like to make you an offer."

Within two weeks, I went from unemployed to chief investment officer at Ankerstar Wealth. Steve needed someone to help build out investment models. He needed someone who could implement a steady system across all risk levels. He needed someone who thought about math and markets the way he did, but could also explain things to clients who weren't math people. That's where I came in.

What Makes Us Different

We're not Wall Street. We're Main Street. We don't wear suits. We're not pompous. We're not trying to impress you with complicated words or fancy charts that nobody understands.

We're real people who've also been on your side of the table. In fact, I've been the client who didn't understand what my advisor was talking about. I have been frustrated by fees I didn't know I was paying. I've been annoyed by advisors who disappeared after getting my money. And I've sat across from people who never bothered to ask what I actually wanted—who skipped past my goals, ignored my current situation, and handed me a cookie-cutter plan that had nothing to do with my life. They weren't partners. They were salespeople who checked in once a year, if that, and never adjusted anything when life changed. I know what that feels like. At Ankerstar Wealth, we've built something different because of it.

First, we believe in relationships. We want you to text us when something's on your mind. We don't want you to call the office and schedule an appointment three months from now. We want to be accessible when you need it most.

Second, we believe in clarity. If we can't explain an investment to you in thirty seconds, we shouldn't own it. Period. No jargon. No hiding behind complexity. Clear thinking leads to clear communication.

Third, we believe in accountability. We meet weekly as an investment team. We meet monthly with our advisory board. We meet quarterly with clients in public meetings that we record and post online. We're not hiding our process because we want you to see how we think.

Fourth, we believe in performance. We've grown 30 to 50 percent every year since we started. We've done this without paying for ads or running marketing campaigns. We've done this because people tell their friends about us.

When clients compliment us, they don't just talk about returns. They say things like, "You've built something special." They talk about the team. They talk about the way we communicate with them. They talk about feeling like they're part of something different.

That's what we're building.

Why We Wrote This Book

This book isn't just about us; it's about a better way to invest.

For too long, the financial industry has been focused on collecting fees instead of serving clients. Advisors sell products instead of building relationships. They make things complicated instead of clear. They disappear instead of staying present.

We know there's a better way.

This book is built around two simple concepts: thesis and conviction. A thesis is our reason for owning something. Can we explain it in thirty seconds? Do we know why this investment makes sense? What would make us sell it? A conviction is how strongly we believe in that thesis. High conviction means a bigger position. Low conviction means a smaller position or no position at all.

Together, these concepts change everything. They take you from emotional reactions to analytical thinking. They give you an anchor during volatility. They help you know when to hold and when to fold.

We use this framework every day, with every investment, and with every client. We've seen it work in bull markets and bear markets alike, in calm times and crazy times.

Now we want to share it with you.

What You'll Learn

You'll find the pages ahead are divided into three parts:

Part one shows you why the traditional approach is broken. We'll walk through the cookie-cutter solutions that don't actually work. We'll show you the fee stacking that drains your returns. And we'll explain why most people don't know what they own or why.

Part two introduces the thesis and conviction framework. We'll teach you how to build a thesis. We'll show you how to assign conviction. We'll walk through real examples from our own investing—both personally and for clients. You'll also see exactly how we think about investments from start to finish.

Part three is about purpose. Investing isn't just about making money—it's about what that money enables. It's about teaching your kids. It's about having options. It's about significance beyond a bank account balance.

Who This Book Is For

This book is for anyone who wants to invest better, whether you're a professional managing client portfolios or a retail investor managing your own. Maybe you're reading articles online, watching YouTube videos, and trying to figure it all out on your own. Or maybe you've been in the industry for years, but you're stuck executing the same tired 60/40 portfolio because that's what everyone else does. Either way, this book will give you a framework that cuts through the noise—one built on conviction and thesis, not on autopilot allocation models that haven't been innovative for decades.

Maybe you're working with an advisor, but something feels off. You don't really understand what you own. Your advisor disappeared after you signed the paperwork, or you're unsure if you're paying too much in fees. This book will help you ask better questions, demand better service, or know when it's time to make a change.

Maybe you're an advisor yourself. You're tired of the cookie-cutter approach, and you want to build real relationships with clients. You want to do work that matters. This book will show you a different way.

Or maybe you're just curious. You heard of this book from a friend and want to know what the buzz is about. That's fine too. Stick with us. We think you'll find something valuable here.

We're going to tell you the truth, even when it's uncomfortable. We're not going to pretend we're always right. We're not going to pretend investing is easy. We want you to invest better, whatever that looks like for you.

Some of what we say might make traditional advisors uncomfortable. That's okay because the industry needs serious change, and we're not afraid to shake things up.

Finally, we're going to keep things simple—no jargon unless we define it first, no complicated charts, no math beyond what a middle schooler can understand. If we can't explain it, we'll keep working until we can.

Let's Get Started

The client who discovered he had $8 million represents one side of financial planning. He's the happy surprise. But most people aren't sitting on hidden wealth. Most people need clarity. They need direction. They need someone to help them organize the financial garage so they can see what they actually have.

That's where thesis and conviction come in.

These two concepts will change how you think about investing. They'll give you confidence during market drops. They'll help you avoid the mistakes that derail most investors. They'll turn you from someone who owns investments into someone who understands investments.

Ready? Let's go.

Your financial future is too important to leave to cookie-cutter solutions, fee stacking, and advisors who ghost you after getting your money. You deserve better, and we're going to show you what better looks like.

Key Points

- Most financial stress comes not from lack of money, but from lack of clarity.

- Stop and ask yourself: Are you making life decisions based on clear financial reality, or on what you hope is true?

Chapter 1:

The Industry Has Lost Its Way

Several years ago, I (Mike) sat down with a high school friend, Richard, at a smoothie shop near his house. We had played football on the same team. We'd also stayed in touch over the years, crossing paths at the gym or local Elks club, and when I started working at Ankerstar, he was one of the first people I called.

"I do invest a little," he told me when we met up to catch up on life. "Actually, I invested in two stocks last year."

"Really?" I said. "How'd it go?"

He made a face. "Well, one of them doubled. But the other one went to zero. Bankrupt."

I leaned back in my chair and smiled, saying, "That's the best thing that could have ever happened to you."

He looked at me like I'd lost my mind. His eyes went wide. "What? How is that the best thing?"

"Because," I said, "they both could have gone to zero. You had no diversification. If you'd picked two bad stocks instead of one good one and one bad one, you would have lost everything. And you probably would never invest again. You'd be so burned by the experience that you'd give up on the whole thing."

He was quiet for a second, processing what I'd just said.

"Or," I continued, "they both could have doubled. Then you'd think your logic was working perfectly. You'd keep doing the same thing, putting all your eggs in one or two baskets, until eventually you'd hit two bad ones in a row and lose everything anyway."

He nodded slowly, starting to see it.

"But this," I said, gesturing with my hands like I was holding something, "this is perfect. You're breaking even. You're coming out with the same amount you started with. And now you're sitting here with me, open to learning a better way. That's why it's the best thing that could have happened."

Richard is still a client today. He's in our aggressive model, which means he takes on more risk than some of our other clients—but it's managed risk. He owns positions that can move up quickly when we're right. However, there is the key difference from his old approach: He's diversified. He's not gambling on one or two stocks anymore. He's invested in a carefully built portfolio, with clear reasons for owning each position. And he's comfortable with it because he understands it.

The Real Problem

Richard's story shows what happens when investing becomes gambling. He had one or two positions, with no real plan, and no understanding of what could go wrong—just hope and excitement. But his story is actually the best-case scenario in the world of bad investing. At least he was trying and taking action. Many people are stuck in something just as bad: cookie-cutter solutions that don't actually work for them.

The financial industry has lost its way. It started with good intentions, back when stockbrokers charged fees per transaction to help people buy and sell individual stocks. That made sense. You were paying for a service. Someone was executing trades for you that you couldn't do yourself.

Fast forward, and technology changed everything. Online platforms made it easy for anyone to buy and sell stocks. The old business model of charging per transaction died, and Wall Street needed a new way to make money.

So they invented mutual funds.[1] Then they invented more mutual funds. Then they convinced everyone that if one fund is good, dozens of funds must be better. They built an entire system based on complexity and fees instead of clarity and results.

The pitch became, "You're not smart enough to do this yourself. You need professionals, and those professionals need to spread your money across dozens of different funds to keep you safe."

But here's what they don't tell you: More funds don't mean more safety. They mean more fees. Every fund has someone managing it. Every manager takes a cut. When you own fifty different funds, you have fifty different people reaching into your net worth and taking their piece of your hard-earned money.

---

1   A mutual fund is when a group of people put their money together to buy investments like stocks and bonds. A professional manager decides what to buy and sell. When you invest, you own a piece of everything in the fund, and you make money (or lose money) based on how well those investments perform.

And what do you get in return? You get performance that usually trails.[2]

My Apple Discovery

I (Steve) learned this lesson the hard way with my own money years ago. I was still in the military, nearing retirement. I knew I wanted to start an investment firm when I got out, so I paid close attention to how the professionals managed money.

I had my money with USAA, which is a company that serves military members. I thought I was being smart. I owned individual shares of Apple because I believed it was the best company in the world. That was my big bet, my personal conviction. And then I had a bunch of mutual funds for diversification and safety.

One day, I looked at what was inside those mutual funds. I wanted to understand what I really owned. So I pulled up each fund and reviewed its top holdings.

Apple was the number one holding in almost every single fund.

I sat there staring at my computer screen, doing the math in my head. I thought I had my Apple position over *here* and my diversified funds over *there*. But I was actually overweight in Apple across my entire portfolio. I didn't know it because it was hidden inside all those different funds.

Now, Apple turned out to be an excellent investment—I'm not complaining about that part! But I had no idea I was so

---

2   Index funds are investment funds that simply copy a market average (like the S&P 500) rather than trying to beat it.

concentrated in one stock. I thought I was being responsible and diversified. Instead, I had a false sense of security. The mutual funds gave me the appearance of diversification without the actual benefit.

That's when I started to get angry, but not at myself. I was angry at the system that made this so complicated that even someone like me, who was studying to become a financial advisor, couldn't see what was really happening.

My Parents' Fifty Funds

The anger got worse when I looked at my parents' investments. They were working with a company that did *only* mutual funds. My parents were so proud when they told me about their investments. "Steve, it's great," my dad said. "We're in fifty different mutual funds."

Fifty.

I asked them to send me their statement. When it arrived, I spread it out on my kitchen table and started going through it line by line. Fund after fund after fund, different names, different ticker symbols, different expense ratios—it all added up to a massive pile of fees.

I called them back. "This is insane," I said. "You have fifty different people reaching into your net worth every single day, taking little fees. They're telling you this is the way to invest. It's not. It's the way for them to make money off of you."

My dad got quiet. He trusted his advisor. He didn't want to believe he'd been sold something that wasn't in his best interest.

"Look," I said, trying to be gentler (emotional sensitivity isn't exactly my strong suit). "These aren't bad people. But this system isn't designed for you, it's designed for them." I knew I could do it in a better way.

That conversation was one of the moments that convinced me I needed to start my own firm. I needed to build something different, something that was actually designed to help clients instead of just collecting fees.

The Relationship Desert

The fee problem is bad enough. But there's something even worse about how most of the financial industry operates: Many financial advisors don't *actually* want a relationship with you.

Here's how it usually works. You meet with an advisor. They're charming. They're interested in your life. They ask about your kids, your job, and your goals. They make you feel heard. They make you feel like they care.

Then you sign the paperwork and transfer your accounts, and they disappear.

You might get a quarterly statement in the mail. You might get a call once a year if they're really on top of things. But mostly, you don't hear from them. Your money is there, somewhere, doing something, but you don't really know what.

Until one day, you start thinking about leaving. Maybe you heard about another advisor. Maybe you're not happy with your returns. Or maybe you feel forgotten.

That's when your advisor suddenly reappears. They call you "out of the blue." They're your best friend again and have all these "new ideas" they want to share with you—ideas that conveniently didn't exist last year when you weren't thinking about leaving.

We see this pattern over and over. A client will tell us they're thinking about moving their accounts to us. We'll say, "Okay, but be prepared. As soon as your current advisor gets that transfer paperwork, they're going to call you. They're going to remind you that you're *best friends*. They're going to have opportunities they haven't mentioned in years."

Sure enough, the call comes. The client tells us later, "You were right. He called the day after I submitted the paperwork. Suddenly, he wants to meet and has all these great new ideas."

That's not a relationship. That's a transaction.

The truth is, the best advisors want actual relationships with their clients. We tell people all the time, "If something is on your mind, text us. Don't call the office and schedule an appointment three months from now. Just text and we'll talk about it."

We archive all our text messages for compliance reasons, so there's a record of everything—but that's not why we do it. We do it because real relationships happen in real time. When you're worried about something at 10 p.m. on a Tuesday, you shouldn't have to wait until your quarterly review to talk about it.

The Knowledge Gap

The traditional model creates another big problem: Clients don't actually know what they own.

Try this experiment. If you're working with a financial advisor right now, call them tomorrow. Ask them to explain one of your investments in thirty seconds. Pick any holding in your portfolio and ask: Why do we own this? What's our strategy with it? What would make us sell it?

If they can't answer clearly and quickly, that's a red flag.

Financial firms train most advisors to avoid these conversations and teach them that their job is to collect assets, put them into model portfolios, and then manage them quietly in the background. Don't bother the clients with details. Keep it simple. Trust us, we're the professionals.

This kind of "relationship" creates a dynamic in which the advisor is "smart," and the client is "dumb" (though that's a false dynamic). The advisor has all the knowledge. The client writes the checks and hopes for the best.

We think that's backwards. We believe clients deserve to understand what they own and why they own it. If we can't explain an investment in language that makes sense, we probably shouldn't own it at all.

I (Mike) have a client who came to me from another advisor with a big firm and a well-known name. When we first met, I asked him what he had invested in.

"I have no idea," he said. "Mutual funds, I think. Some bonds maybe. I really don't know."

"Have you ever asked your advisor?"

"Yeah. He says it's complicated, he's managing it, and I should trust the process."

That's not good enough. Your money isn't that complicated. And if it is, something's wrong.

The COVID Test

In March 2020, the world was falling apart. The pandemic was spreading. Governments were locking down entire countries. Nobody knew what was going to happen next. Were we all going to die? Was the economy going to collapse? Should we sell everything and go to cash?

The market dropped 37 percent in just a few weeks.[3] People were terrified. They weren't just scared about their health, they were scared about their money.

I (Steve) was running the firm by myself at this time. I had a handful of clients and an intern, Jaden, who helped me in the office. The phone was ringing constantly. Emails were flooding in. Everyone wanted to know the same thing: What do we do?

So I started making daily YouTube videos—sometimes even twice a day. I'd get up in the morning, look at what was happening in the markets and the news, and I'd make a short video explaining my thoughts. My goal was to hit three topics in nine minutes.

I gave them titles that captured the moment, like "Blood in the Streets" and "Hold the Line." I was trying to give people something to hold onto when everything felt like it was falling apart.

I told them the truth: My blood's in the street too. I'm not immune to what's happening either. I feel it just like you do, but

---

3 Liz Frazier Peck, "The Coronavirus Crash of 2020, and the Investing Lesson It Taught Us," *Forbes*, February 11, 2021, https://www.forbes.com/sites/lizfrazierpeck/2021/02/11/the-coronavirus-crash-of-2020-and-the-investing-lesson-it-taught-us/.

here's what the data says and what I think we should do.

The market kept falling. Every day, it felt like it could be the day everything went to zero. But I kept crunching the numbers. I kept thinking about what was really happening versus what people feared was going on.

On March 23, 2020, I made a video called "Lock and Load." I told everyone: It's time. This market has opportunity. We're buying.

Turns out, I was just one day early. The actual bottom was March 24, but I was close enough. And the clients who listened and stayed with me through the fear made massive returns over the next year as the market had a historic run-up and to the right.

That was the moment a lot of people really understood what we do differently. It's not primarily about having the perfect timing; it's about having a steady hand when everyone else is panicking. It's about being there with clear communication when everyone else is running for the exits.

Years later, I hired an advisor named Corey. In our first meeting, he said something that stuck with me.

"I've been following you for years. I remember your COVID videos like 'Lock and Load.' You nailed it."

I had no idea he'd been watching. He wasn't even a client then, but he was following along, learning, watching how we handled the crisis. And when he decided he wanted to become a financial advisor himself, he came to us.

That's the power of showing up during the hard times because that's when relationships are strengthened, and trust is forged.

What You Deserve

Here's what should be normal in this industry but somehow isn't:

You should know what you own. It's not just the account balance, but the actual investments—what stocks, what funds, what bonds. You should be able to name at least your top five holdings.

You should understand why you own each position. You don't need complicated financial jargon, just simple language. What's the reason this is in your portfolio? What problem is it solving? What opportunity is it capturing?

You should have a clear exit strategy. For each position, you should know: What would make us sell this? What has to change for this to no longer make sense? These details shouldn't be a mystery.

You should have a real relationship with your advisor. This is not quarterly statements mailed to you. It's not annual reviews where they talk at you for thirty minutes. You deserve a real relationship where you can reach out with questions and get real answers.

You should participate in the upside when things go well. Fee stacking can eat up so many of your returns that even when the market does great, your account barely moves. That's not okay.

You should avoid the downside of complexity and confusion. Investing doesn't have to be complicated. If your portfolio requires a PhD to understand, something's wrong.

These aren't unreasonable expectations. This is just what good service looks like. But somehow, the industry has convinced people that this level of service is too much to ask for. Instead, you should be grateful for the quarterly statement and the annual phone call.

We don't accept that. And you shouldn't either.

The Real Cost

Let's go back to Richard, the former gambler with the two stocks we talked about earlier. When we first sat down, he thought his gambling approach was investing—two stocks, all or nothing. He got lucky with a break-even result. But he could have easily lost everything.

The traditional cookie-cutter approach isn't as dramatic as Richard's story. You probably won't lose everything, but you might lose something just as valuable: The opportunity to build a portfolio that provides financial freedom.

When you're paying fees to fifty different fund managers, those fees compound against you over time. A one-percent fee doesn't sound like much. But over thirty years, it can cost you hundreds of thousands of dollars in lost growth.

When you're in lifecycle funds that automatically get more conservative as you age, you might be giving up decades of growth potential. These funds assume you can't handle volatility. They move you into bonds in your fifties, even though you might live another forty years—which is forty years of missed opportunity!

When you don't have a real relationship with your advisor, you might make emotional decisions at exactly the wrong time. You might sell at the bottom because you're scared, and nobody's there to talk you through it. You might miss the recovery entirely.

The cost of the traditional approach isn't always obvious. It's not like someone stealing money from your wallet. It's subtle. It's the returns you don't get, the growth you miss, the opportunities that pass you by while you're stuck in outdated models.

Richard learned this early, thanks to his two-stock crash-and-burn experience. Most people learn it much later, if at all. Some people go their whole lives not realizing how much the traditional approach costs them.

Moving Forward

I (Mike) still work with Richard. His portfolio looks completely different now than it did when we first met. He's in our aggressive model, which means he takes on more risk than someone close to retirement. But it's a smart risk. It's calculated. It's based on clear reasoning.

When a stock we'd just invested in dropped 30 percent in the first week, I called him right away. I didn't hide from it. I didn't wait for him to call me angry.

"Hey," I said. "I need to tell you something. The position we just bought dropped 30 percent this week. Earnings came out, and they missed the mark. But here's the thing: My thesis hasn't changed. My conviction in this company hasn't changed. So I have three options for you."

I laid them out clearly. We could sell and take the loss. We could hold and wait for it to recover. Or we could buy more because I believed it was now on sale.

"What do you think?" I asked.

He didn't hesitate. "I'm in. Buy more."

The stock was e.l.f. Beauty Inc. It not only recovered, but it also skyrocketed. Richard made money on that position because he trusted the relationship and our process, even when things looked bad in the moment.

That's what good advising looks like. That's what the industry should be doing: clear communication; real relationships; honest assessments; staying present during the hard times, not just the good ones.

What You Need to Know

The financial industry isn't going to change overnight. The big firms are too invested in the current model. They make too much money from fees and complexity. And they benefit from keeping clients in the dark about what they really own.

But you don't have to accept it. You can demand better. You can ask harder questions. You can find advisors who actually want relationships instead of just assets under management.

Or you can learn to do it yourself. You can build your own understanding of what makes a good investment. You can develop your own decision-making framework. You can take control of your financial future instead of handing it over to someone who might not have your best interests at heart. It takes time to learn how to invest, and you may not have the time or energy for this endeavor.

That's what the rest of this book is about. We're going to show you a different way—a better way. It's a way that's based on clarity instead of confusion, on relationships instead of transactions, on performance instead of just collecting fees.

We're going to teach you about thesis and conviction.

These two concepts will change how you think about every investment. They'll give you a framework for making smart decisions, helping you avoid the mistakes that trap most investors.

But first, we had to show you why the traditional approach doesn't work. You have to understand what's broken before we can show you how to fix it.

Richard's story had a happy ending because he was willing to admit that his strategy was reckless and that he had adopted a lottery mentality. Thankfully, he was willing to change course.

The question is this: Are you?

The traditional approach will keep taking your money as long as you let it. Cookie-cutter solutions will keep underperforming as long as you accept them. Advisors will keep ghosting you as long as you tolerate it.

You deserve better. Your family deserves better. Your future deserves better. And in the next chapter, we're going to show you exactly what *better* looks like.

Key Points

- Complexity isn't a feature of good investing; it's a shield used to hide fees and mediocrity.

- Advisors who vanish during calm markets and reappear only when you try to leave aren't advisors—they're salespeople.

- Most investors don't lose because markets crash—they lose because no one was there to guide them through it.

- Stop and ask yourself: When markets fall, do you know in advance what actions you'll take—or do you wait to see how scared you feel in the moment?

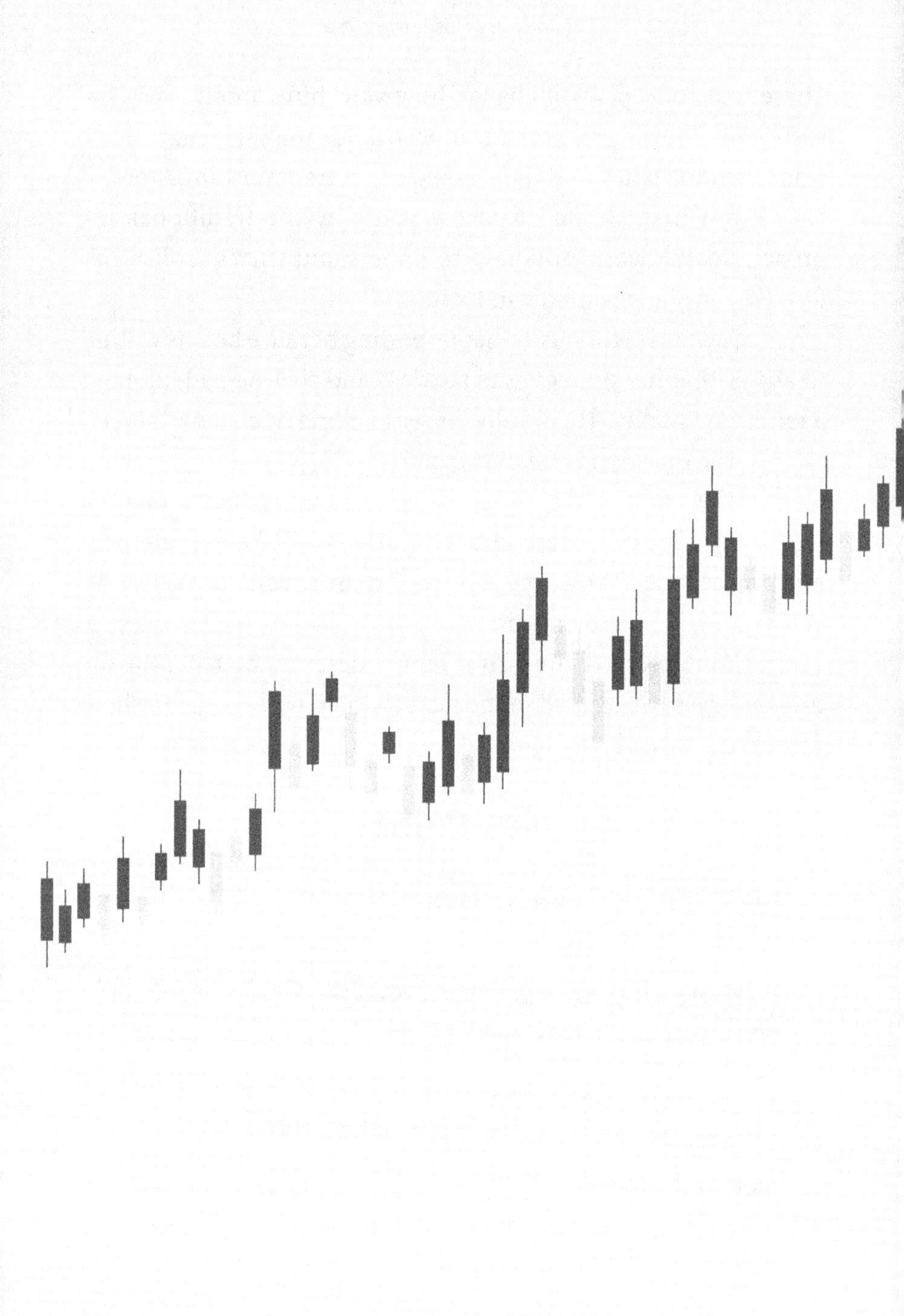

Chapter 2:

Thesis and Conviction

I (Mike) made one of the biggest investing mistakes of my life in my living room. I was sitting at my computer, staring at my brokerage account, feeling relieved. I had just sold all my Netflix shares at $12 each. I was getting out with a tiny profit after months of stress and doubt.

Back then, Netflix mailed DVDs to your house. Remember those red envelopes? I loved getting them. I'd order a movie online, and a few days later it would show up in my mailbox—no more driving to Blockbuster, no more late fees. It was perfect.

I loved the service so much that I bought the stock. This was before I worked at Ankerstar Wealth, back when I was managing my own investments. I bought Netflix in my IRA at $11 per share. I thought I was making a smart long-term bet on a company I believed in.

Then the stock started dropping. The $11 became $10, then $9, then $8. It kept falling until it hit $4 per share. I had lost more than 60 percent of my investment.

I talked to a friend about it. He's a smart guy, and I trusted his opinion.

"The problem with Netflix," he said, "there's no moat. Blockbuster can just copy what they're doing. They can mail DVDs too; nothing is stopping them."

That made sense to me. Blockbuster had stores everywhere. They had brand recognition and relationships with the movie studios. If they decided to compete seriously with Netflix, they could probably wipe them out.

So when Netflix finally climbed back up to $12, I was just happy to get out. I sold everything, feeling like I'd dodged a bullet. I'd gotten my money back plus a tiny bit more. It was time to move on to something less stressful.

Then I watched Netflix go to $50, then $100, then $200, then $500. In early 2025, it was over $1000 per share. If I'd kept my original investment, it would be worth more than one hundred times what I paid for it.

I think about that trade all the time. Not because I'm beating myself up over it, though that's tempting. I think about it because it taught me one of the most important lessons in investing: you need more than a thesis—you need conviction. You need to know the difference between your thesis being tested and your thesis being wrong.

What Is a Thesis?

A thesis is your reason for owning something. It's the answer to a simple question: Why is this investment in my portfolio?

Most people can't answer this question clearly. They own mutual funds because their advisor told them to. They own stocks because they read an article somewhere. They own bonds because someone told them they should at their age. But if you press them for the actual reason, for the real logic behind the investment, they come up empty.

A good thesis has a few key characteristics. First, you should be able to explain it in thirty seconds or less. If you can't explain it on an elevator ride, you probably don't understand it well enough. Second, it should be forward-looking. You're not investing in what happened last year. You're investing in what you think will happen in the future. Third, it should be specific enough that you know what would disprove it.

Let me give you an example. My original Netflix thesis was simple: people hate driving to video stores and paying late fees. Netflix solves this problem by mailing DVDs directly to your house. Over time, more people will use this service, and the company will grow.

That was a good thesis. It was clear. It was specific. It was based on a real problem and a real solution. My problem was that I abandoned it the moment things got hard.

The Thirty-Second Rule

I (Steve) learned about the importance of clear explanation when I was a flight instructor in the Air Force. There's a big difference between being able to do something and being able to teach it to someone else.

When you're an operator, you can get by on instinct and experience. You've done something a thousand times just because you can do it. But when you have to teach someone else, you have to break it down into steps. You have to understand not just *what* you're doing, but *why* you're doing it that way.

I remember trying to teach a student pilot how to land a plane.

"Just drive it down to the runway and then flare right before you touch down," I said. "Don't let it smash into the ground."

The student looked at me like I was speaking a foreign language. "Okay, but when do I flare? How do I know when I'm about to touch down? Where should my eyes be looking?"

I realized I couldn't actually explain it. I'd been doing it for so long that I just felt it. But feeling isn't teaching. I had to go back and think through every single element of landing. Where are your eyes looking? What are your speeds? What are you feeling in the controls? What does the runway look like at each point in the approach?

Once I could break it down like that, I could teach it. The same thing applies to investing. If you can't explain your investment thesis in thirty seconds, using language that a middle schooler would understand, you probably don't understand it well enough yourself. If you don't understand it, you definitely shouldn't be risking your money on it.

Good Thesis Examples

Let's look at a few examples of good investment theses. As of early 2026, these are positions we actually own at Ankerstar Wealth, and we can explain each one clearly.

Apple

Apple is a luxury brand that happens to make technology products. Their customers are locked into their ecosystem with phones, computers, watches, and services that all work together seamlessly. This creates incredible customer loyalty and allows Apple to charge premium prices with premium profit margins. We would sell if their ecosystem advantage disappeared or if their brand became less desirable to consumers.

Bitcoin

Bitcoin offers an alternative to government-backed currencies at a time when governments are spending beyond their means and printing money to cover the difference. With a fixed supply of $21 million coins and growing acceptance by institutions and countries, it functions as digital gold. We would sell if governments successfully banned it, if a superior alternative emerged, or if the debt and money-printing problems that make it attractive somehow got solved.

Palantir

Palantir's AI-powered software helps governments and large companies make sense of massive amounts of data. Their government contracts, especially for national security and counter-terrorism, create a strong moat and reliable recurring revenue. We would sell if competitors matched their capabilities at lower prices or if government spending on data analytics significantly decreased.

Notice what these theses have in common. They're all clear. They're all based on something specific the company does or provides. And they all include a clear idea of what would make us sell.

Bad Thesis Examples

Now let's look at some bad theses. These are things we hear all the time from investors who don't really have a decision-making framework.

"It's undervalued."

Okay, but it's undervalued compared to what? And when does it become fairly valued? If your whole thesis is that something is cheap, you have to sell when it's no longer cheap. Most people who buy based on value never actually sell. They just hold forever and hope.

"Everyone's talking about it."

The statement above is momentum investing disguised as a thesis. It might work in the short term, but it's not a reason to own something long-term. When everyone stops talking about it, what happens then?

"It went up yesterday."

Past performance is not a thesis. It's just a description of what already happened. You need a reason to believe it will continue going up in the future.

"My friend recommended it."

Unless your friend is Warren Buffett, this isn't due diligence. You need to understand the investment yourself, not just trust someone else's opinion.

The problem with all these bad theses is that they don't provide a framework for making decisions later. When the stock drops, what do you do? When it goes up, when do you sell? Without a real thesis, you're just guessing.

The Thesis as Your Anchor

Here's where the thesis becomes powerful. When you have a clear reason for owning something, you have an anchor during volatility. The stock price bouncing around doesn't matter as much because you're focused on the underlying business and whether your thesis is still valid.

The question changes from "What's the stock price today?" to "Has the thesis changed?" That's a huge shift in mindset. It takes you from emotional reactions to analytical thinking.

Consider Rocket Labs. In February 2025, the stock sat around $28. By April, tariffs and market fear had dragged it down to $16—a gut-wrenching 43 percent drop. The noise was deafening. Is the world fundamentally different now? Have we lost this opportunity for good?

This example is exactly where the thesis earns its keep. Instead of panic-selling, we went back to our original reasoning. We re-examined the fundamentals. We asked the hard questions. And when we looked at everything honestly, the answer was clear: The thesis hadn't changed. The opportunity was still there. So we held. Some of us bought more.

That doesn't mean the next four months were comfortable. They weren't. We had to sit through the uncertainty as the price languished. At the same time, everyone else questioned whether tech stocks would ever recover. But by June, Rocket Labs had climbed back to its previous highs. And then it kept going—eventually quadrupling from that April low.

Here's the thing: We didn't hold on blindly. We actively pressure-tested our conviction. When the price dropped, we didn't just shrug and hope for the best—we went back to the thesis and made sure we all still agreed it was intact. That's the difference between disciplined investing and wishful thinking.

What Is Conviction?

Now let's talk about the second pillar: conviction. This is how strongly you believe in your thesis. It's the difference between thinking something is a good idea and believing something is a great idea.

Conviction determines position sizing. If you have high conviction, you take a larger position. If you have low conviction, you take a smaller position or no position at all. It sounds simple, but most investors do it backwards. They size positions based on emotions or arbitrary rules rather than on how much they actually believe in the investment.

I (Steve) learned about conviction from flying fighter jets. Every time you take off in a single-seat fighter, you're betting your life that you assessed the risks correctly. You've checked the airplane. You've reviewed the mission. You've planned for contingencies. Now you have to decide: Am I confident enough to launch?

On March 21, 2003, I faced that question in the starkest terms possible. I was about to drop the first bomb of Operation Iraqi Freedom—the opening strike of shock and awe.[4] I'd be going in first, alone, in a stealth platform. With no one ahead of me to clear the way, it was just me, the aircraft, and everything I'd trained for.

In that moment, conviction wasn't abstract; it was the difference between launching and not launching. I had to trust my training. I had to trust the airplane. I had to trust my fellow squadron pilots who would execute their parts of the mission. All of that preparation, all of those contingencies we'd planned— it all came down to one decision: Do I believe in this enough to act?

I did, and the mission was successful.

That's conviction. It's not just having a thesis about whether something will work. It's being willing to act on that thesis with real stakes on the line.

In investing, conviction works the same way. The stakes aren't life and death, but the mindset is identical. I'm not easily moved off my thesis. I'm not sidelined by turbulence or noise. I've done the work, checked the fundamentals, and planned for contingencies. When I commit, I stay with the plan and see it through.

---

4 "Largest Air Campaign in U.S. Military History—Shock and Awe," YouTube video, 9:18, posted by HistoryMarathon, April 20, 2018, https://www.youtube.com/watch?v=23P4AAz-BqHY.

Conviction in Practice

Let me show you how this plays out in real life. At Ankerstar Wealth, we have different conviction levels for different investments across our team. This difference is actually healthy. It creates checks and balances. It prevents any one person's overconfidence from creating too much risk.

Take quantum computing as an example. I (Steve) have a very high personal conviction in quantum computing. I believe it's going to be a revolutionary technology that changes everything, as much as the internet did. I'd personally be comfortable with a large position. But other members of our team have lower conviction. They think quantum computing might be too early. They worry we could be years away from practical applications and see it as a solution looking for a problem.

So what did we do? We took the team's collective conviction and sized the position accordingly. Quantum computing currently accounts for about 2 percent of our most aggressive models. That's a real position. We're participating. But it's not so large that it would hurt badly if we're wrong or if we're just too early.

As quantum computing develops and we see more evidence, our collective conviction might increase. Then we'd increase the position size. Or our conviction might decrease if we learn things that challenge the thesis. Then we'd reduce or exit the position. The point is that position size matches conviction level, and conviction level changes as we get new information.

How Thesis and Conviction Work Together

Here's the key insight that ties everything together. Thesis tells you what to own; conviction tells you how much to own. You need both.

A thesis without conviction is just an idea. You might think something is a good investment, but if you're not willing to put real money behind it, it doesn't matter.

Conviction without a thesis is just gambling. You might feel really strongly about something, but if you can't articulate why, you're betting on emotions instead of analysis.

When you have both, everything changes. You know what you own and why you own it. You know how much to own based on how strongly you believe in it. You have a framework for making decisions when things get volatile, and you can explain your thinking to other people in clear language.

Having both thesis *and* conviction is what separates professional investors from amateurs. Amateurs buy things because they seem exciting or because someone told them to. Professionals have clear theses and calibrated conviction for every position they take.

But here's the uncomfortable truth: most so-called professionals don't operate this way either. Walk into the average financial advisor's office and ask them why they own a particular fund. You'll get vague answers about diversification, asset allocation models, or whatever the home office recommended this quarter. They're not building theses. They're following playbooks written by someone else.

The mutual fund industrial complex has trained an entire generation of advisors to distribute products, not to think. They'll put you in a basket of funds, rebalance once a year, and call it a strategy. But ask them to articulate a real conviction about a specific position. Ask them to explain exactly why they believe in something or what would have to change for them to sell. Most can't do it. They've never had to.

What we do—and what only a handful of others do—is different. Every position has a thesis. Every thesis has been pressure-tested. Every one of us can tell you exactly why we own what we own and what would make us change our minds. That's not the industry standard; that's the exception.

The Netflix Lesson Revisited

Let me (Mike) go back to my Netflix story from the beginning of this chapter. Now you can see what I did wrong.

My thesis was actually good. Netflix solved a real problem in a way that customers loved. That thesis didn't change when the stock dropped from $11 to $4. The company was still mailing DVDs. Customers still loved the service. The fundamentals hadn't changed.

What changed was my conviction. I let the stock price movement shake my belief in the company. When my friend pointed out that Blockbuster could copy the model and make them irrelevant, I let that doubt override my original thinking. My conviction collapsed, so I sold.

Here's what I should have done. I should have asked myself: Has the thesis changed? Is Netflix still solving the same problem? Are customers still using the service? The answer to all those questions was yes. The stock price was down, but the company was still executing on its winning plan.

If my thesis hadn't changed, I should have held. Or better yet, I should have increased my position by buying more—the stock was on sale! Everything I initially believed about Netflix was still true. In reality, Blockbuster's attempts to compete validated that Netflix was onto something important. But I didn't have the framework then that I have now. I didn't understand the difference between a thesis being tested and a thesis being wrong. So I sold at exactly the wrong time and missed out on one of the best investments I could have made.

I learned from that mistake. Now, when I see positions drop, I don't panic. I ask: Has the thesis changed? If the answer is no, we hold or buy more. That's conviction in action.

What This Means for You

You don't need to be a professional investor to use your thesis and conviction. You can apply this framework by holding your financial advisor accountable. Ask them about each investment in your portfolio. What's their thesis? Can they explain in thirty seconds why you own it? If they can't articulate a clear answer, that's a warning sign. Pay attention to their conviction. Do they sound confident in the reasoning, or are they just repeating what they were told to sell? If your advisor can't quickly explain why you own something and express genuine conviction about it, you might be holding investments for bad reasons or no reasons at all.

Then ask about their conviction. On a scale of one to ten, how confident are they in each thesis? Are your position sizes matched to their conviction levels? Are you over-allocated to things they're not that sure about? A good advisor should be able to give you honest answers about where they have high conviction versus where they're less confident.

Finally, set a schedule for these thesis and conviction reviews with your advisor. Once a quarter is good for most investors. Ask them: Has anything changed? Have you learned something new that increases or decreases your conviction in this position? Should we be adjusting position sizes? These conversations will tell you whether your advisor is actively managing with intention or just leaving things on autopilot.

This framework won't guarantee there will never be mistakes. I still think about my Netflix trade and wonder what could have been. But using thesis and conviction will give you a systematic way to make decisions instead of just reacting to emotions or following the crowd.

That's the power of thesis and conviction. These two things working together turn investing from an emotional guessing game into something logical and organized. They give you confidence during volatility and clarity during uncertainty. They help you know when to hold and when to fold.

In the next chapter, we're going to show you how to build your own theses by looking forward instead of backward. Because the best investments aren't found by looking at what happened yesterday. They're found by identifying what's coming tomorrow.

Key Points

- An investment you can't explain in thirty seconds isn't so-phisticated—it's reckless.

- Big positions without clear reasoning are gambling, no matter how confident you sound.

- Volatility exposes weak thinking long before it destroys capital.

- Stop and ask yourself: When volatility hits, do I default to a process—or do I default to emotion?

Chapter 3:

The Strategy of Forward-Looking Investing

I (Steve) started my stock-picking career with a spectacular failure. In high school, we had a class called Essentiology. It was one of those rare classes that actually teaches you valuable things about life: how to balance a checkbook; write a resume; understand car insurance; and, for one project, the basics of investing.

To get some hands-on experience with investing, we each had to choose a stock and track it for the semester. I picked Pier One Imports (I don't even remember why). Maybe I liked their furniture. Maybe my mom shopped there. Whatever the reason, I thought it was a sure thing.

As in everything, hindsight is twenty/twenty, and it wasn't the homerun I'd anticipated. Pier One took a major nosedive. By the end of the semester, I was one of the worst performers in the class, so much for my career as the next Warren Buffett.

But here's what I learned from that experience. I had no idea what I was doing. I picked Pier One based on a whim, an emotional reaction, a gut feeling. I didn't understand their business. I didn't know their competition. I didn't have any real reason to think they would do well. I just picked a name I recognized and hoped for the best. That's not investing. That's guessing, and the market has a way of punishing serial guessers.

The problem was simple: I was looking backward. I picked Pier One because I knew about it. I wasn't thinking about where the furniture industry was going. I wasn't asking whether their business model made sense for the future. I was looking at what was in front of me and making a bet.

Real investing requires looking forward. You're not betting solely on what happened yesterday. You're betting on what is probable to happen tomorrow. And the investors who do this well are the ones who can see changes coming before everyone else does.

The Three Questions

To do this effectively, you must learn to identify themes. A theme is not merely a short-term trend or a fad; it is a fundamental structural shift in how the world operates. It is a massive tailwind created by necessary change. To spot these themes before the rest of the market does, you have to know where to look. We use a simple framework to find them.

Over the years, I've developed three questions that help me identify potential investment themes. These questions force me to think forward rather than backward. They push me to seek change and disruption rather than buy what's comfortable and familiar.

Question One: What problems need solving?

The biggest investment opportunities usually come from solving big problems. Not every problem is equal. Some problems are annoying but manageable. Other problems could break an entire system if they aren't fixed. Those are the ones you want to find.

Think about the national debt. Right now, in early 2026, the United States owes about $38 trillion (and growing).[5] That's not a small problem. That's a system-breaking problem if it doesn't get addressed. How do you get out of that? Historically, countries have tried austerity measures, but nobody wants to cut spending. They've attempted to grow their way out, but the debt is growing faster than the economy. They've tried printing money, but that causes inflation.

What if there was another option? When governments are in a debt spiral, their primary move has been to print more money to cover the difference, which inevitably debases the currency and erodes your purchasing power. But what if you could opt out? What if instead of using money that governments can manipulate, people started using money that nobody controls—money backed by math rather than politicians, with a fixed sup-

---

5   Joint Economic Committee, Republicans, "National Debt Hits $38.43 Trillion, Increased $2.25 Trillion Year over Year, $8.03 Billion Per Day," news release, January 9, 2026, U.S. Congress, https://www.jec.senate.gov/public/index.cfm/republicans/2026/1/national-debt-hits-38-43-trillion-increased-2-25-trillion-year-over-year-8-03-billion-per-day

ply that can never be diluted? That's the Bitcoin thesis in a nut-shell. It's a solution to a massive problem that doesn't have any good traditional answers.

Question Two: What could be more efficient?

Some of the best investments come from finding things that take too long, cost too much, or waste too many resources. That's why you look for companies or technologies that can do those things better, faster, or cheaper.

Think about household tasks. For hundreds of years, humans have done their own cooking and cleaning. Then we got some appliances that helped, like dishwashers and washing machines. These made everyday tasks more efficient, but they had a limit: You still had to operate them. You still had to load the dishwasher. You still had to push the vacuum.

The next leap in efficiency isn't just a better tool; it's removing the human operator entirely.

Imagine a world where labor is treated like a utility. Right now, if you want your car washed, you either do it yourself or drive to a car wash, wait in line, and crawl through. But what if there was a task-based app—like Uber for chores? You pull out your phone, tap the "wash car" button, and see a price of $4. You accept. A robot arrives, washes your car perfectly, and then leaves for its next job.

You don't have to own the robot. You don't have to maintain it. You pay a fraction of the cost for the specific task you need done, without leaving your home. That is a massive efficiency gain. It takes the friction out of daily life. It solves labor shortages by deploying machines that can work twenty-four hours a day without needing sleep or breaks. That technology is coming in the next few years, and it will change the economic equation for everyone.

Question Three: What does the next generation need?

Young people today face different problems than their parents did. They have different expectations. They use different tools. They think about work, money, and life differently. If you can understand what they need, you can find investment opportunities before most people even realize those needs exist.

I (Mike) think about this a lot. The average age for buying a first home is now forty years old.[6] That's up from around thirty years old just a generation ago. Young people are getting priced out of homeownership. They're spending twenty years as renters before they can afford to buy.

What does that do to their psychology? What does that do to their goals and dreams? Instead of saving for a house, they decide to invest differently. Instead of focusing on the physical world, they spend more time in digital spaces. Maybe property in the metaverse becomes more appealing when you're stuck in a small apartment you don't own.

---

6   National Association of REALTORS®, "First-Time Home Buyer Share Falls to Historic Low of 21%, Median Age Rises to 40," November 4 2025, https://www.nar.realtor/newsroom/first-time-home-buyer-share-falls-to-historic-low-of-21-median-age-rises-to-40.

I'm not saying this is good. I'm saying this is what's happening. And if you can see these trends before everyone else, you can position yourself to benefit from them.

Learning From Movies and Books

One unconventional source of forward-thinking ideas is entertainment. Movies and books imagine futures that don't exist yet. Some of those futures seem ridiculous. However, some of them turn out to be quite prophetic.

Think about *Star Trek*. It imagined wireless handheld communicators in the 1960s. Now we all have smartphones. It imagined a computer you could talk to and ask questions, and now we have Siri, Alexa, and ChatGPT. It dreamed of a world where people from different countries and backgrounds worked together in space. (We're not quite there yet, but we're getting closer).

Or think about *Minority Report*. It showed people controlling computers by waving their hands in the air. That seemed ridiculous when the movie came out. Now we have gesture controls and virtual reality that work exactly like that.

I (Steve) grew up reading science fiction. Not casually—aggressively. As a child, I devoured everything I could get my hands on—Asimov, Clarke, Heinlein, and whoever else was on the library shelf. At the time, it was just for the joy of it. I didn't realize I was training my brain to do something that would prove invaluable decades later: imagine futures that don't exist yet.

Science fiction expands your sense of what can happen. It takes ideas that seem absurd today and plays them out to logical conclusions. Sometimes, buried in those stories, you find investment ideas before the rest of the world catches on.

When I watched *Ready Player One*, I didn't just see entertainment. I saw a possible future—one where digital worlds become as important as physical ones, where people live and work and build identities inside virtual spaces. Most viewers left the theater and forgot about it by dinner. I walked out thinking about which companies were building the infrastructure for that future. Virtual reality hardware, gaming platforms, digital ecosystems—these are the building blocks of a world that doesn't fully exist yet but might.

Now, movies and books won't give you specific stock picks. That's not how this works. But they can help you spot themes earlier than others. They can make you comfortable with ideas that seem weird or impossible to everyone else—ideas that most investors will dismiss until it's too late to capture the real upside.

In investing, being early to a theme is where you make the most money. As John Maynard Keynes said, "Successful investing is anticipating the anticipations of others." Science fiction taught me how to anticipate.

From Theme to Thesis

Finding an investment theme is just the first step. Once you've identified a big problem, an efficiency opportunity, or a generational shift, you need to turn that into an actual investment thesis. That means getting specific about who's positioned to win and why.

Let's revisit the robot example. The theme is clear: Robots will make tasks more efficient and give people back their time. But that's not specific enough to invest in yet; you need to answer some more questions.

Who's building these robots? What companies are technologically ahead? Do they have a real product or just a concept? How much will it cost? When will it actually be available to consumers? What could go wrong?

Right now, Tesla is one of the leaders with their Optimus robot. They've shown prototypes that can walk, use tools, and complete tasks. Boston Dynamics has robots with incredible movement capabilities. Several other startups are working on this as well. The race is on, and we don't know yet who will win.

So how do you invest in this theme? You could buy Tesla stock, but you're also buying their car and energy business. You could try to invest in private startups, but that's risky and not available to most people. Or you could look for companies that supply the parts or the AI that powers these robots.

The point is that you start with the theme and then you do the work to figure out the specific investment. You build a thesis that says, "I believe humanoid robots will be a huge market. Based on my research, I think Company X is best positioned to capitalize on this. Given my conviction, I'm willing to invest Y percent of my portfolio on this thesis."

Now, let me tell you a story about one of my early wins. It shows how thinking one level deeper than everyone else can pay off.

The Ambarella Lesson

In 2014, GoPro cameras were everywhere. Every skier had one mounted on their helmet. Every cyclist had one on their handlebars. Every adventure traveler had one recording their trips. The X Games were a thing. The stock was hot. Everyone was talking about buying GoPro.

But by the time everyone's talking about a stock, it's usually too late. The easy money has been made. I looked at GoPro and thought, "This is a craze. Crazes are dangerous to invest in directly, but maybe I can invest around the craze."

So I started digging. What makes a GoPro work? Who supplies the technology?

I found out that a company called Ambarella made the chips that powered GoPro cameras. They had an exclusive contract, and every GoPro used an Ambarella chip. Ambarella's stock hadn't grown nearly as much as GoPro's had. Nobody was talking about it yet. To me, it was a hidden opportunity.

I bought Ambarella for clients. The stock went up significantly over the next year. We eventually sold it and took profits. My original clients still talk about the "Ambarella trade" as one of the legendary wins from the early days of the firm.

The lesson isn't "always invest in suppliers." As in chess, the lesson is "think one level deeper than everyone else." When there's a craze, look at who benefits. When there's a trend, look at who's providing the infrastructure. When there's a theme, look at all the ways to invest in it, not just the obvious one.

The Advantage of Clients

One of our biggest advantages at Ankerstar Wealth is our access to hundreds of households filled with smart clients. These aren't just people we manage money for. They're business owners, entrepreneurs, professionals, and experts in their fields. They see trends in their industries before those trends make the news.

I (Steve) tell our advisors all the time, "Listen to your clients." They're going to tell you about investment opportunities if you pay attention. They're not trying to give you stock tips. They're just talking about their work and their lives. But if you listen carefully, you'll hear themes emerging.

A client who runs a manufacturing company talks about how they're starting to use AI to optimize their production line. That's a data point. Another client who works in healthcare talks about how they're implementing AI to help diagnose patients. That's another data point. A third client who owns a restaurant talks about how they're using AI to manage inventory and reduce waste. That creates a pattern.

When you hear the same theme coming from different industries, that tells you something big is happening. That's how we spotted AI as a major theme before it became apparent to everyone else. It's not because we're geniuses, but because we listen

You don't need hundreds of clients to do this. You need to pay attention to the world around you. Talk to people about their work. Ask questions about what's changing in their industry. Read widely across different fields. Look for patterns that connect different things. The best investment themes are usually hiding in plain sight. You have to be looking for them.

When to Act

Here's the tricky part about forward-looking investing. If you wait until everyone agrees with you, you're too late. The stock has already moved. The opportunity is gone. But if you're too early, you can lose money for years while you wait for your thesis to play out.

The phrase I use is "I would rather be wicked early than late." That means I'm willing to be wrong about timing if I'm right about the direction. I'm willing to buy something that doesn't move for a while. I'm willing to sit through periods where people mock me for being in something that hasn't worked yet.

Take my earlier conviction about quantum computing. I've had high conviction in quantum computing for a few years now. Other members of our team think I'm too early. They believe the technology is ten or twenty years away from being practical. They might be right about the timing. Here's my thinking. If quantum computing happens, and it's as revolutionary as I think it will be, being early costs me some opportunity today, since I'm not investing that money in other positions. However, being late costs me the entire opportunity. I'd rather pay the price of being early than pay the price of missing it entirely.

That doesn't mean you should put 50 percent of your portfolio in speculative themes. It means you take a small position early and increase it as your conviction grows. You participate enough to benefit if you're right, but not so much that it kills you if you're wrong or too early.

This example is where conviction and position sizing come back into play. High conviction with uncertainty about timing means a modest position. High conviction with certainty about timing means a large position. Low conviction means a small position or no position. The framework keeps you disciplined when you're making forward-looking bets.

What You Can Do

Thinking forward in your investments is mission-critical. The good news is that you don't need to be a tech expert or a futurist to think this way. You need to ask the right questions and pay attention to the answers.

Start by asking: What problems do I see in the world that need solving? Don't just think about your personal problems; think about systemic issues that affect millions of people. The problems that could break things if left unfixed are the ones that create the biggest opportunities.

Then ask: What could be more efficient? What takes too long? What costs too much? What wastes resources? Look for companies or technologies that could dramatically improve these things.

Finally, ask: What does the next generation need that my generation didn't? How are their lives different? What challenges are they facing? What opportunities are they chasing? The answers point you toward long-term trends that most people are missing.

Once you have a theme, do the research. Who's positioned to win? What companies are ahead? What could go wrong? Build a specific thesis, not just a vague idea, and be willing to act even if other people think you're crazy. Some of the best investments seem crazy until they become obvious.

In the next chapter, we're going to dive deep into our biggest forward-looking bet: Bitcoin. You'll see exactly how we went from skeptics to believers. You'll understand the complete thesis development process from start to finish. And you'll learn how we manage a position that's now our largest holding across most of our client portfolios.

Bitcoin isn't just an investment for us, it's a case study in how to build conviction in something that most people still don't understand.

Key Points

- Buying what you recognize or what worked in the past isn't investing—it's nostalgia with money attached.

- Ignoring how the next generation lives is a guaranteed way to miss the next wave of growth.

- Being early feels uncomfortable, lonely, and wrong—right up until it becomes obvious and everyone pretends they saw it coming.

- Stop and ask yourself: How differently does the next generation live, work, and spend compared to my generation?

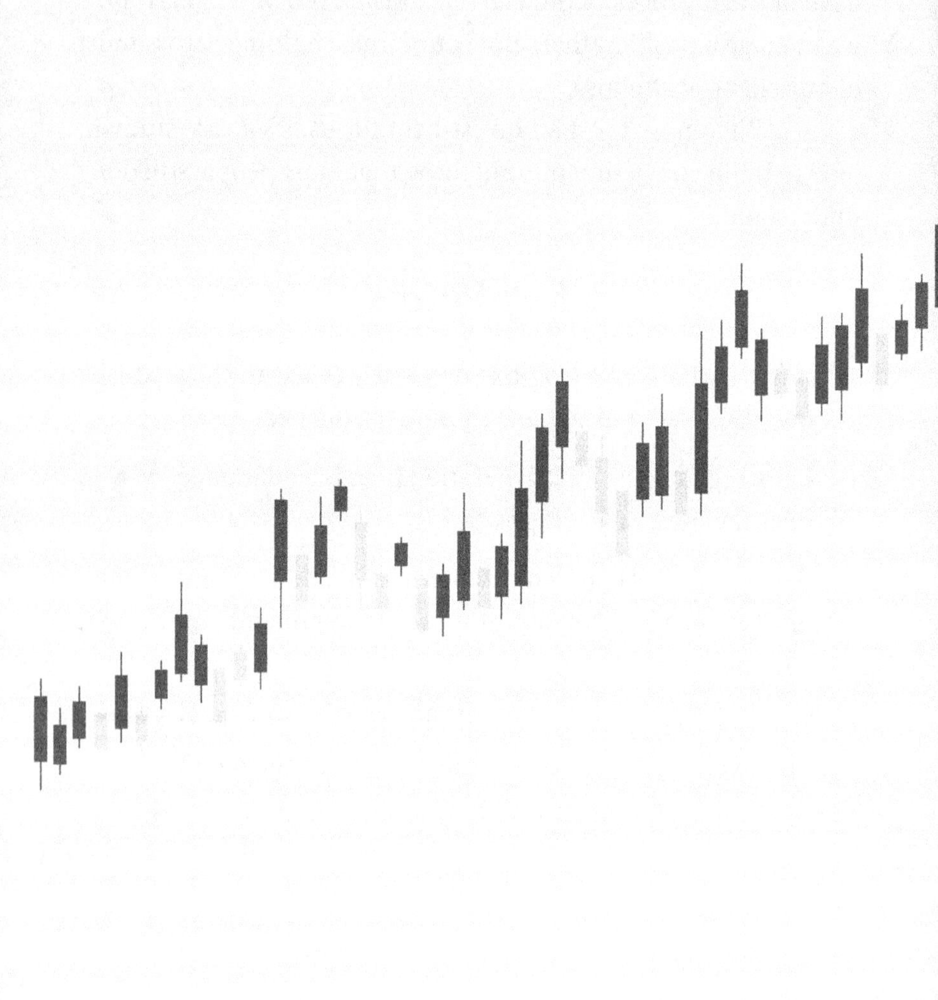

Chapter 4:

All In

I (Mike) picked up the phone and called my client Ben. It was the day Bitcoin crossed $100,000. The news was everywhere, with every financial website running the headline. People who had never thought about Bitcoin were suddenly talking about it.

Ben is a retired CEO. He's a smart guy with a successful career. But he's not someone who pays close attention to the details of his portfolio. He trusts us to manage it, and he doesn't look at it very often. That's good with us. That's what we're here for.

"Hey Ben," I said. "Did you hear the news? Bitcoin crossed $100,000."

"Yeah," he said. He was at a golf course with some friends. I could hear them talking in the background. "We were just talking about that. Pretty wild."

"You know you own it, right?"

There was a pause. "What?"

"You own Bitcoin. We've had it in your portfolio for a while now."

Another pause. Longer this time. "Are you serious?"

"Totally serious. It's part of the model we put you in. You've been participating in this whole run-up. It's not a huge percentage of your account, but enough to make a real difference."

I could hear him processing this information. Then I heard him turn to his golf buddies. "Guys, apparently I own Bitcoin." There was some commotion. His friends had been talking about Bitcoin as if they'd missed out on it. Now Ben was telling them he'd been in it the whole time without even knowing.

"Keep telling your friends," I said with a smile. "You're not sitting on the sidelines. You're in the game."

That conversation captures an important aspect of how we approach Bitcoin at Ankerstar Wealth. Ben didn't have to research Bitcoin, cryptocurrencies, or blockchain technology himself. He didn't have to decide whether to buy it. He didn't have to time the market or stress about whether it was too late. We did all that work for him. We built the thesis. We developed the conviction. We sized the position appropriately for his risk level. He got to benefit from it without any of the anxiety.

That's what this chapter is about. It's not just Bitcoin as an investment, but Bitcoin as a case study in how thesis and conviction work in practice.

From Mockery to Curiosity

I (Steve) first heard about Bitcoin in 2010. The movie *The Social Network* had just come out, and the Winklevoss twins were talking about this new digital currency they were investing in.

My reaction was immediate and dismissive: This was the dumbest idea I had ever heard. Money that isn't backed by a government? Money that only exists on computers? That's not money. That's a joke.

I (Mike) felt the same way. The only context I had for Bitcoin was criminal activity. Drug dealers used it on the dark web. Hackers demanded ransoms in Bitcoin. Why would any legitimate person want to be associated with that?

We both ignored Bitcoin for years. It would pop up in the news occasionally, usually because the price had crashed or because some exchange had gotten hacked. Each headline confirmed what we already believed. Bitcoin was a speculative bubble and was going to zero eventually. So the smart play was to stay away.

Then something started to shift. I (Steve) was doing interviews for my YouTube channel in 2020, trying to learn about different investment topics. One of my clients knew a Bitcoin expert and offered to connect us. I wanted to learn more about Bitcoin because I had dismissed it until that point, but it was gaining real traction. So I reached out to learn about what I might be missing.

I asked him every hard question I could think of. How is Bitcoin unhackable when everything digital gets hacked eventually? What's the actual use case beyond speculation? Will any government actually let this threaten their currency? And what about all the criminal activity?

His answers were detailed and thoughtful. But honestly, I didn't understand most of what he said because I didn't have enough background knowledge to process it. The interview ended; I thanked him for his time and filed it away in my memory as "interesting but probably not relevant."

Two years later, I went to a digital assets conference in Austin, Texas. Digital currency experts Ric Edelman and Josh Brown were speaking. Both were respected financial advisors with long track records. If they were taking Bitcoin seriously, maybe I should pay more attention.

The Candy That Changed Everything

Ric Edelman did something at that conference that finally made the blockchain click for me (Steve). He pulled out a piece of candy and held it up.

"I'm going to ask a simple math question," he said. "If you think you know the answer, shout it out. Ready? What's seven times six?"

Many in the audience yelled, "Forty-two!"

Ric pointed at her. "I heard her first. She gets the candy." He walked over and handed it to her. Everyone was watching, not sure where this was going.

"Now," Ric said. "What if she had said forty-nine? How many of you would have spoken up to correct her?"

Every hand in the room went up.

"That's how the blockchain works," he said. "Everyone is watching. Everyone is checking. If someone tries to record a wrong answer, everyone else immediately knows. You don't need a bank to verify transactions. You don't need a government to guarantee the money. You need a bunch of people who are all paying attention and who all benefit from keeping the system honest."

I sat there stunned. For years, I had heard explanations of the blockchain that made no sense to me. Hash rates, proof of work, distributed ledgers—and none of it clicked. But the candy analogy was so simple that even a child could understand. Suddenly, I got it.

The blockchain isn't just a database with rows of transaction history. It's a system where cheating is basically impossible because everyone is watching everyone else. Every transaction is visible to everyone (which means millions of people). If someone tries to fake a transaction, thousands of other computers immediately flag it as wrong. You'd have to fool more than half of all the computers in the network at the same time to cheat the system. Fooling that number of computers is essentially impossible.

The Reading Assignment

Josh Brown spoke next. He talked about where Bitcoin fits in a portfolio and how advisors should approach it. But the thing that stuck with me was his homework assignment.

"If you want to understand Bitcoin, you need to read *The Bitcoin Standard*," he said. "It's about three hundred pages. It explains everything. And if I see you at the next conference and you haven't read it, I don't want to talk to you."

That night, I found the document online and read the whole thing. It laid out the case for Bitcoin in clear, logical terms. Here's the argument in simplified form.

Governments around the world are spending more money than they collect in taxes. To cover the difference, they print more money. This process is called monetary expansion, or quantitative easing, or various other technical terms. The effect is simple: each dollar becomes worth less over time. That's inflation.

For most of history, money was backed by gold. You couldn't just print more of it. But in 1971, the United States went off the gold standard. Since then, the money supply has expanded dramatically. A dollar today buys a fraction of what it bought in 1971.[7]

Bitcoin offers an alternative. There will only ever be 21 million Bitcoin. That number is fixed in the code and cannot be changed. No government can print more Bitcoin. No central bank can expand the supply. It's based on math and baked-in accountability, rather than trust in institutions.

If you believe that governments will continue spending beyond their means, and if you believe they'll continue printing money to cover the gap, then Bitcoin makes sense as a hedge. It's digital gold, a store of value that political decisions can't debase.

I read that document and thought, "This actually makes sense." I still had questions and doubts swirling in my mind. But for the first time, I understood the thesis—and it was compelling.

From Understanding to Action

Six weeks after that conference, I started buying Bitcoin for client portfolios. We started with 13 percent in our most aggressive models. That was already higher than almost any other advisor was doing. Most firms were at zero. A few adventurous ones were at 1 or 2 percent. We came in at 13 percent because our conviction was high.

---

7   Nick Lioudis, "Understanding the Gold Standard: History, Collapse, and Impact on the U.S. Dollar," Investopedia, updated November 3, 2025, https://www.investopedia.com/ask/answers/09/gold-standard.asp.

Then we waited. Bitcoin is famous for its volatility, and we experienced it firsthand. The price would surge, then crash (a pattern likely to continue, though the overall movement is up and to the right). Clients would get nervous. We'd explain the thesis, then the price would surge again. It was a rollercoaster.

But here's the key: The thesis never changed. Governments kept spending. Debt kept growing. Money printing continued. Everything that made Bitcoin attractive in the first place was still true. So we held.

January 11, 2024, was a big day: The SEC approved Bitcoin exchange-traded funds (ETFs) for the first time.[8] Now we could use actual ETFs that tracked Bitcoin's price directly, with lower fees. It had better tracking and was easier to trade. We moved client money into the new ETFs immediately.

Then Bitcoin started its next big run. It had been around $40,000 at the start of 2024. By the end of the year, it crossed $100,000. Our clients were making serious money on their Bitcoin positions.

The Decision Not to Sell

Here's where it gets interesting from a thesis and conviction standpoint. Standard portfolio management says you should rebalance. When one position grows much larger than your target allocation, you're supposed to sell some and buy other things. That keeps your risk balanced. We didn't do that with Bitcoin, at least not right away.

---

8   "Bitcoin ETFs Begin Trading on U.S. Exchanges, Posting Gains on First Day as Crypto Prices Rise," *CNBC*, January 11, 2024, https://www.cnbc.com/2024/01/11/bitcoin-etfs-begin-trading-on-us-exchanges-posting-gains-on-first-day-as-crypto-prices-rise.html

Why? Because our conviction hadn't decreased. If anything, it had increased. Bitcoin was doing exactly what we thought it would do. Institutional adoption was growing. More companies were putting Bitcoin on their balance sheets. More countries were exploring it. The thesis was playing out in real time.

So instead of selling Bitcoin down to 13 percent, we raised our most aggressive target allocation to 18 percent. We let our conviction drive the decision instead of following a mechanical formula. We were saying, "We believe in this even more now than we did before. Why would we sell something we believe in more?"

Building the Comprehensive Strategy

I (Mike) started thinking about how to bring Bitcoin to clients who couldn't stomach the full volatility. An 18 percent position in something that can drop thirty points in a week isn't for everyone. Some of our clients are naturally conservative. Others don't want that level of stress.

In early 2025, new products came out that offered Bitcoin exposure with downside protection. These are structured products that use options to limit your potential losses. In exchange, they also limit how much you can gain. But for conservative investors, that tradeoff makes sense.

One product offers protection at 20 percent down. That means if Bitcoin drops, the most you can lose is 20 percent. In exchange, your upside is capped at 50 percent. If Bitcoin doubles, you only get 50 percent of that gain. But if Bitcoin crashes 60 percent, you only lose 20 percent.

Another product is even more conservative. It protects you at 10 percent down with a 30 percent upside cap. And there's one that's basically principal-protected. You can't lose money, but your upside is limited to around 11 percent.

We used this information to create what we call a comprehensive Bitcoin strategy. Now we could offer Bitcoin exposure across all risk levels. Aggressive clients get full volatility. Moderate clients get a blend of full exposure and protected positions. Conservative clients get mostly protected positions. Everyone can participate at their own comfort level.

Ben, the client I called when Bitcoin hit $100,000, was in one of our moderate models. He had Bitcoin exposure, but it was partially protected. He got to participate in the upside without taking the whole rollercoaster ride. That's why he could be on a golf course, not even thinking about his portfolio, while his Bitcoin position was growing.

The Question That Haunted Me

I (Steve) went to another conference in March 2025. Ric Edelman was hosting again. We were having a conversation in a small group, and he said something that stuck with me for weeks.

"Are we doing our clients a disservice?" he asked. He was talking about advisors who personally hold 50 percent or more of their wealth in Bitcoin but only recommend 5 or 10 percent to clients. "If we believe in it that much for ourselves, but we tell clients to keep their positions small, is that really serving their best interests and meeting our fiduciary obligations?"

That question haunted me. My personal portfolio was about 90 percent Bitcoin at that point—you could say I'm extremely bullish. I had studied it deeply. I believed in the thesis completely. But I was telling clients to hold at 18 percent at most. Was that inconsistent?

After thinking about it for a month, I came to a conclusion. Different people have different risk tolerances and levels of understanding. What's right for me isn't necessarily right for a seventy-year-old retiree who wants to make sure she doesn't run out of money. Professional money management means considering each client's situation, not just imposing my own views on everyone.

But we should also offer options for people who want more Bitcoin exposure, who understand the thesis, and have the risk tolerance and the time horizon. Jack Mallers captured this perfectly when he said, "Anyone who understands Bitcoin doesn't take 1 percent of their portfolio and use it as a hedge. Anyone who understands Bitcoin, Bitcoin is like their entire portfolio." That resonated with me. There are people out there who get it at that level. Why weren't we serving them?

So in May 2025, we created Bitcoin-only models. When I wrote the internal memo announcing them, I felt like I was making history. Bitcoin had just moved from $77,000 to $104,000 in a matter of weeks. A 35 percent surge that was noticed worldwide. Bitcoin Treasury Companies were popping up rapidly. More people were paying attention to and learning about Bitcoin than ever before. I believed we were on the cusp of a historic move higher, and I wanted our clients to have the option to participate fully if they shared that conviction.

These Bitcoin-only portfolios are 100 percent focused on Bitcoin and related investments. They're not for everyone. They're not even for most people. But for someone who understands the thesis and wants concentrated, professionally managed Bitcoin exposure, we now have that option.

The key is that clients can choose. Someone with $1million could put $900,000 in a traditional diversified portfolio and $100,000 in a Bitcoin-only model. They're getting concentrated Bitcoin exposure on part of their money while keeping most of their wealth diversified. It's about giving people options that match their convictions.

Reaching a New Generation

I (Mike) was at a conference in Miami when I met someone who would change how we think about our business. His name was Aaron Langley, and he was one of the founders of a company called Autopilot.

The week before, my wife had told me to listen to a podcast. Tucker Carlson was interviewing the CEO of Autopilot about something called the "Pelosi Tracker." It's a model that follows the stock trades that Nancy Pelosi reports to the government. Whatever she buys, the model buys, and it's done really well over the years.

I listened to the podcast and found it interesting. Then I'm at this conference in Miami, talking to random people, and Aaron mentions he's one of the Autopilot founders. I couldn't believe it, I had just been learning about his company.

We talked for a while, and he explained what Autopilot does. They enable people to subscribe to investment models through their phones. You connect your trading account, pick a model you like, and the trades happen automatically. When the model manager makes a change, your account is updated with the same change within minutes.

That got me thinking. We have all these models at Ankerstar. What if we made them available on Autopilot? We could reach investors we'd never have met otherwise. Young people on their phones. People who aren't going to call a financial advisor and schedule a meeting. People who want professional investment management but want to access it through an app.

I came back and pitched it to Steve. He was skeptical at first. It was a new platform and a different business model. He wasn't sure it would work. But we tried it. We put our Bitcoin models on Autopilot. Then we added models for quantum computing, humanoid robotics, and other themes we believe in. Traction started growing—fast. We started with four core portfolios, and have now grown to fourteen thematic portfolios listed on Autopilot.

These portfolios are built for people who want a digital experience, not a traditional one. They want to hop in on their own terms, do their own research, move funds quickly, and invest in what they believe in—all without waiting on phone calls or sitting through meetings. They're self-directed by nature.

When we look at where the next generation of investors is heading, this is it. They've grown up managing everything from their phones. The traditional wealth management experience doesn't fit their lifestyle. We want to be positioned in front of those investors before they start looking for a home.

Where We Think It's Going

Let's talk about the future. That is where the thesis really matters, because we're not just investing in what Bitcoin is today. We're investing in what we think it will become.

Right now, Bitcoin functions primarily as a store of value. People buy it and hold it, hoping it will be worth more in the future. That's similar to gold. You don't use gold to buy groceries; you hold gold as a hedge against uncertainty. Bitcoin has the potential to become more than that. It could become actual money that people use for everyday transactions. Not Bitcoin itself, because one Bitcoin is worth too much for buying a cup of coffee. But Satoshis, which are tiny fractions of Bitcoin, are small enough to use like dollar bills.

Imagine traveling to another country in the future. Instead of exchanging dollars for the local currency, you spend Satoshis directly. The merchant accepts them because they're worth the same everywhere. No exchange rates. No bank fees. No government can freeze your funds or devalue your money.

The biggest obstacle is governments. Governments like controlling their currency. It lets them manage the economy, fund spending through money printing, track transactions, and collect taxes. Bitcoin threatens all of that.

Here's our view. The problems that make Bitcoin attractive aren't going away. Governments aren't going to become fiscally responsible suddenly. The national debt isn't going to shrink magically. Money printing isn't going to stop. As long as those problems remain, Bitcoin has a reason to exist. And as more people understand that, adoption will grow.

What This Means for You

You don't have to invest in Bitcoin to learn from this chapter. The Bitcoin story is really about how to develop conviction in something that most people don't understand or don't believe in.

We started as skeptics. We thought Bitcoin was a fad at best, but we kept learning. We went to conferences and read the foundational documents. We asked hard questions. We challenged our own assumptions. Eventually, our views shifted because the evidence changed them.

That's how conviction should work. It's not blind faith or following the crowd. It's continuous learning and honest assessment of what you're seeing. Sometimes you learn things that increase your conviction. Sometimes you learn things that decrease it. The key is staying open to new information and being willing to change your mind.

This sounds simple, but it isn't. Human nature pulls us toward what we already believe. We flock toward information that confirms our biases and away from anything that challenges them. It's comfortable. It's also dangerous, especially when real money is on the line.

I (Steve) learned this lesson formally when I earned my third master's degree. One of the most valuable things that the program taught me had nothing to do with the subject matter itself. It was about how to educate yourself honestly.

Here's how it worked: We had to write a one-page proposal for a semester-long paper, carefully laying out our case for a particular position. I spent a month crafting my argument, marshaling evidence, building what I thought was an airtight thesis. Then came the twist. The next assignment was to write an equally rigorous counter-argument for a position I didn't believe in.

That exercise changed how I think. It forced me to seek out information that I disagreed with. To look for kernels of truth in opposing views. To actively hunt for challenges to my own thesis instead of avoiding them.

Most people don't do this. They build a case for what they already believe and stop there. Here's the truth: You're never going to prove your thesis unless you seek out challenges to it. The positions that survive honest scrutiny are the ones worth holding. And once a thesis survives that scrutiny, conviction demands you do something about it.

We also showed you how conviction translates into action. We didn't just say "Bitcoin is interesting," we sized our positions based on how strongly we believed. Then, as our conviction grew, we raised our allocations, created new products to serve different client needs, and expanded into new platforms to reach new people.

That's what thesis and conviction look like in practice. You're not just having opinions. You're acting on them in proportion to how strongly you believe.

Key Points

- Conviction is meaningless unless it shows up in real portfolio decisions.

- True fiduciary responsibility means aligning recommendations with belief, evidence, and client reality.

- Hiding behind diversification to avoid hard choices is not risk management—it's fear management.

- Stop and ask yourself: When I look back ten years from now, will I regret being too aggressive—or being too cautious when the evidence and belief was clear?

Chapter 5:

The Speedboat and the Cruise Liner

I (Steve) like to use an analogy when people ask why we operate the way we do. Imagine you are out in the middle of the ocean. To your left, you see massive cruise liners. These are the huge institutional firms like Vanguard and BlackRock. The ships are enormous, with twelve swimming pools and a buffet line that stretches for a mile. They also have a problem.

If the captain of that cruise liner sees an iceberg ahead, or perhaps a beautiful tropical island he wants to visit, he turns the rudders—then he waits. It takes five miles for that ship to actually make the turn. By the time the ship responds, the opportunity is gone. Or the iceberg has already torn a hole in the hull.

Now look at us. We are a speedboat, zipping between these massive ships. When we see an opportunity, we turn the wheel, and the boat turns immediately. If we realize we need a correction, we can turn back just as fast. We can throttle up; we can throttle down. Today, where the pace of change is accelerating faster than anything we have seen in history, you do not want to be stuck on a cruise liner. You want to be on the speedboat.

The Fallacy of "Buying the Haystack"

The financial industry has spent the last forty years convincing you that you are safer on the cruise liner. They call it "passive investing." The marketing pitch is seductive.

They tell you: "Don't try to beat the market. Just buy the market." They tell you to buy the S&P 500 index fund. "Buy the SPY and die," as the saying goes. The logic is that if you buy the whole haystack, you are guaranteed to find the needle. And statistically, that is true.

If you own the S&P 500, you own the winners. You own Apple. You own NVIDIA. But here is the part they don't say loud enough: You also own all the dry, dead grass. You are intentionally putting your hard-earned capital into hundreds of companies that are dying. You are buying companies that haven't innovated since the 1980s. You are purchasing retail chains that Amazon is crushing. You are buying legacy car companies that can't figure out EVs.

Why would you do that?

I challenge advisors all the time with what I call the Pepsi Challenge. I ask them: "Can you name thirty of the five hundred companies in the index you just sold your client?" They can't. They don't know what they own. This mentality—"we are smart, you are dumb, so just buy what we tell you"—is insulting. It assumes you can't handle the truth about what is actually happening in the economy.

No one has time to learn about five hundred different companies. We would rather pick the best basket of stocks because we want the needles, not the hay. We want to filter out the noise. We want to eliminate the companies without a compelling thesis or strong conviction. This is because, over time, owning quality is safer than owning mediocrity.

No Partial Credit

I (Steve) developed this mindset long before I was a pilot or an advisor. It started at Iowa State University. I was an engineering student. We called the program the "Hate Factory." They were trying to weed us out. The professors had a brutal philosophy: no partial credit. In most college courses, if you get the answer wrong but you show your work and your logic is sound, the professor gives you a C or maybe a B for effort, but not in engineering. My professor would say, "If you build a bridge and you get the math 90 percent right, but you miss one strut, the bridge falls. People die. That is an F. You don't get a 90 percent because the bridge looked pretty before it collapsed."

It was harsh. It sent many students packing. But it taught me that results matter more than process. The big cruise liner firms *love* process. They love committees and compliance reviews that take six months. If a young advisor at a big firm has a great idea—say, investing in Quantum Computing—he has to fight through three levels of bureaucracy. He has to get it on the agenda for the quarterly meeting. If he missed the deadline, he has to wait two months. That is the speed of bureaucracy. That is the process. They get an A for process. If the market moves while they are having their meetings, the client gets an F on the result. We don't accept partial credit. We don't want to be right in theory; we want to be right in your account balance.

The Monday Morning Quarterback

I (Mike) deal with the other side of this equation. Steve is the strategy guy looking at the horizon. I'm the one talking to the clients who are feeling every bump in the waves. A few months ago, my wife, Trisha, had to have heart surgery. It was a scary time. We met with the surgeon beforehand. He was confident and clearly explained the procedure. Several friends gave me great advice. They said, "Mike, do not go on Google. Do not watch videos of heart surgery. Do not try to be an expert." They said, "The surgeon is not going to call you from the operating room to ask for your advice."

I took that advice to heart and trusted the surgeon. I didn't stand in the operating room shouting, "Hey, maybe you should make the incision two inches to the left!" That's called "Monday Morning Quarterbacking", and in medicine, it's ridiculous. But in investing, people do it all the time.

You have a phone in your pocket, and because you can see the scoreboard every second of the day, it is tempting to think you should be calling the plays. I recently had a client's teenage son call me. He's enthusiastic and just getting started on his investing journey. He has about $700 in an IRA. He called, sounding panicked.

"Mike, my account is down huge," he said, almost out of breath.

My stomach dropped. I thought, *Did I miss something? Did the market crash while I was at lunch?* I pulled up his account on my screen.

"It's down $14," I said.

"Yeah, I'm really nervous."

I took a breath. Then said, "Okay. I am glad you are sharing that with me. Mathematically, that is a 2 percent drop. That is a normal Monday in the market." But I also told him: "It is good you are feeling this now, because $14 on $700 feels bad. But someday, this will be a $700,000 account. And a 2 percent drop on that will be $14,000. It's the same math, but the emotion will be a thousand times more intense."

We want you to be involved. We want you to understand the thesis. But at some point, you have to let us go to work for you. You chartered a speedboat. You don't need to take the wheel and tell us how to navigate the waves. Which, for even the most skittish of investors, is a relief once they realize the boat is in the hands of wise, informed, and capable sailors.

The Rebalancing Trap

One of the biggest differences between the "cruise liner" approach and our approach is how we handle winning. Traditional portfolio management is obsessed with rebalancing. The computer flags an account and says, "Alert! Your Apple stock has gone up. Your bonds have gone down. You are out of balance." So the textbook answer is sell the winner (Apple) and buy the loser (bonds) to get back to your forty/sixty split. Academically, you get an A plus for that. Your professor would be so proud. In the real world, you just sold your best horse running full speed to buy a donkey that is limping.

I (Steve) tell people: "Rebalancing is often just code for selling winners to buy losers." What is there to like about that statement? Nothing. When we see a winner running—whether it's a tech stock or an asset like Bitcoin—we don't automatically chop its head off just because it hit a certain percentage. We let it run.

Recall our Bitcoin positions. We didn't start with an 18 percent allocation target. Instead, we bought it. It went up, and it kept going up (with fluctuations, of course).

The "cruise liner" rulebook says trim it back. But we looked at the thesis and asked, "Has the thesis changed?" No. So we changed the model to match the performance. We raised the ceiling instead of lowering the asset. We let the winner turn into a strong position because the thesis was still playing out.

Now, we aren't reckless. Eventually, a position gets so big that it becomes a risk management issue. When Bitcoin hits that 18 percent threshold in our aggressive models, we do trim. We don't want to fall victim to our own biases. We don't want one asset to swallow the whole portfolio. But we spend most of the journey letting it grow, rather than constantly cutting it down to size.

Our "War Room"

So how do we make these decisions? We don't wait for a quarterly board meeting in a mahogany room. We meet weekly. Every Friday morning, the entire investment team gets together. We are debating. We are pitching ideas. If an advisor sees something—

say, a position is looking undervalued—they bring it to the table. We debate it. If the thesis is strong, we move. We moved into a position once and held it for six months. It didn't grow. We debated it again. And it turned out the capital was dead, so we got out. We pivoted back out as fast as we pivoted in.

In addition to our weekly internal meetings, we have an Investment Advisory Board (IAB) meeting monthly. This meeting includes our advisors, as well as partners in the firm—clients who own shares of Ankerstar Wealth. These are smart people: business owners, entrepreneurs, and leaders in their field. We put our ideas in front of them so they can punch holes in our theories. It holds us accountable and saves us from operating in an echo chamber. And then once a quarter, we have a public meeting. We broadcast it live, then put it on YouTube. We want you to see the kitchen. We want you to see how the meal is made. We want you to "watch us cook."

We aren't hiding our process, because we want you to see how we think. This structure allows us to be the speedboat. We don't have to ask permission from a headquarters in New York. We don't have to wait for the bureaucracy to catch up to the market. Today, the market is moving too fast for permission slips.

Taking Swings

I (Mike) was new to Ankerstar Wealth when I pitched Steve on an idea. I called it EGO—Exponential Growth Opportunities. The concept was simple: Identify ten small-cap or mid-cap companies that we believed could double or triple within a year. They weren't blue chips or safe bets. They were companies with real upside potential based on clear thesis.

Steve agreed, and from day one, EGO has been wildly successful.

The key is that these weren't gambles. They were thesis-driven bets. Each company had a clear reason for being in the portfolio. We could explain in thirty seconds why we thought it would grow and what would have to happen for us to be wrong. The conviction was there. We just needed the courage to act on it.

That's something I've learned about Steve over the years. He's willing to back people who have conviction. If you can articulate your thesis clearly, if you can explain why you believe what you believe, he'll give you room to execute. He's not looking for people who play it safe. He's looking for people who think clearly and act decisively—true critical thinkers.

That's the culture we've built at Ankerstar Wealth. We take swings—not reckless swings, not throwing darts at a board—calculated, thesis-driven swings where the risk-reward ratio makes sense. Sometimes we're wrong. Sometimes a position doesn't work out the way we thought it would. But we'd rather be wrong occasionally while taking intelligent risks than be "safe" while missing the opportunities that create real wealth.

When the Thesis Plays Out

Of course, not every thesis works out the way you hope. Part of being a good investor is knowing when to walk away.

We had a position once where the thesis was crystal clear. The economic trajectory looked promising. We did our homework, built our conviction, and moved in.

Then nothing happened.

Week after week, we'd look at the position in our Friday meetings. "Is the thesis still valid?" Yes. "Has anything changed fundamentally?" No. "Is it moving?" Not really.

For six months, the capital just sat there—dead money. The thesis remained intact, but the position wasn't performing. Everything we believed was still true, but the market wasn't rewarding us for being right.

Eventually, we decided to exit. Not because the thesis was wrong, but because the risk-reward ratio had shifted. We'd been sitting in this position for half a year with nothing to show for it. That capital could be deployed elsewhere, in opportunities that were actually moving. The thesis can remain valid while still not being the best use of your money.

A situation like this is one of the hardest lessons in investing. You can be right about something and still need to move on. Being right isn't enough—you need to be right at the right time, with the right timeline. If the market isn't going to recognize the value you see within a reasonable timeframe, sometimes the smart move is to take your capital elsewhere.

We pivoted back out as fast as we pivoted in. That's the speedboat advantage we talked about earlier. We don't have to ride a dead position for years because some committee approved it, and nobody wants to admit it's not working. We can move. We can adjust. We can redeploy.

The thesis is essential, but it's not sacred. It's a tool for making decisions, not a cage that traps you in positions that aren't performing.

The cruise liners are safe and comfortable. They will get you to the same destination everyone else is going to. If you want to be average, if you want the same returns as your neighbor, by all means, buy the "haystack." Pay the fees to fifty different managers. Rebalance your winners into losers. But if you want to go somewhere different—if you want to capture the growth of the future—you need a vehicle that can turn.

Key Points

- Size creates inertia—and inertia kills opportunity in fast-moving markets.

- Owning everything means accepting the winners and funding the losers.

- Smart investing requires taking calculated swings, not hiding behind averages.

- Stop and ask yourself: If the world is changing faster than ever, why am I invested as if nothing ever changes?

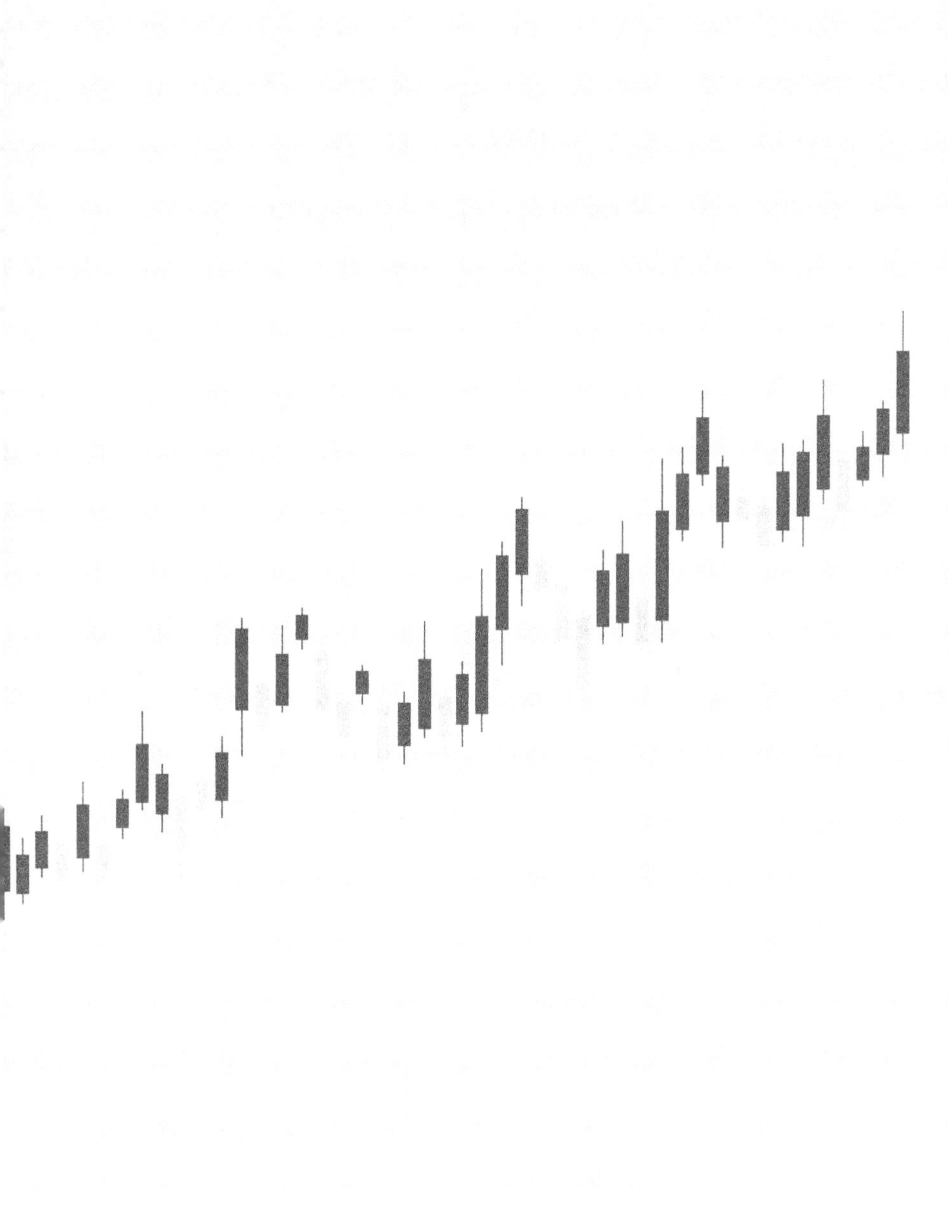

Chapter 6:

Beyond Returns

I (Steve) should have died on May 11, 2013. It was the Saturday before Mother's Day. I was in Ohio, about to fly an experimental aircraft that my dad had spent years building. My mom had called me in tears a few weeks earlier, worried that my dad was going to kill himself trying to fly this thing. So I drove up from Mississippi to fly it first. I had more experience. I had twenty-five hundred hours of flight time in military jets. If anyone could handle whatever surprises this plane had in store, it was me.

Or so I thought.

We spent the afternoon doing ground tests, checking temperatures, checking RPMs, making sure everything was working. My dad and his buddy followed me in a minivan as I taxied out to the runway, watching for fuel leaks or anything else that looked wrong. The sun was getting low, and we were running out of daylight.

I got clearance from the tower and started my takeoff roll. I called out my speeds on the radio so they could track everything. Thirty knots. Fifty knots. Seventy knots. Eighty-two knots, rotation. Ninety-two knots, airborne.

I was about thirty feet off the ground when the engine quit.

Now, engine failures happen. Pilots train for them constantly. The procedure is simple: nose down, maintain airspeed, glide to a landing spot. I'd practiced this a thousand times—no big deal. I pushed the stick forward to start my glide.

But the airplane didn't respond the way it should have. My dad had painted the plane a few times, and paint is heavier than most people realize. The extra weight in the tail had shifted the center of gravity too far back. Instead of gliding, the plane basically fell out of the sky. The bottom dropped out, and there was nothing I could do about it.

Time does strange things in moments like that. Everything slowed down. I remember being angry. Not scared, just furious. I had flown combat missions. I had been shot at. I had survived situations that would make most people's hair turn white. This was how I was going to die? In an experimental plane crash in rural Ohio?

I thought about my wife and my two daughters. I thought about all the things I still wanted to do. Then, in a moment I still can't fully explain, I accepted it. I resigned myself to dying. I slammed the stick to the side, hoping to hit wing-first instead of nose-first, and I slumped in my seat.

That slump probably saved my life. Like a drunk driver who survives a crash because they don't tense up, my body went limp right before impact. The plane hit the ground and broke apart around me. Somehow, I ended up lying face-down in the grass, covered in what I thought was fuel but turned out to be blood from my broken face.

Source: Journal-News[9] | Image credit: Andy Crawford

I pulled myself out from under the wreckage, stood up, and looked back at what was left of the airplane. It was unrecognizable. Then I started walking toward the end of the runway, thinking I was the star of my own action movie. At some point, I decided I should probably take a knee. The next thing I knew, I was velcro-strapped to a bodyboard and being loaded into an ambulance.

The injuries weren't as bad as they could have been. Broken face. Internal bleeding from where the control stick hit my stomach. A huge gash across my forehead from my glasses. The doctors kept me in the ICU for a few days for observation.

---

9   Eric Schwartzberg, "Man Injured in Plane Crash," *Journal-News*, May 12, 2013, https://www.journal-news.com/news/man-injured-plane-crash/UNChCQBDfpbzRwxoYAvvhK/

The next morning was Mother's Day. I called my wife to tell her what happened. She was in New Mexico at the time. I was supposed to be in Mississippi. Neither of us was in Texas, where we were about to buy a house.

The day after that, Monday, I was supposed to close on that house remotely. I called my realtor from the ICU. "Can we move the remote closure to Ohio?" I asked. He said, "Sure, no problem," and asked for the address. I gave him the hospital address and room number. He didn't seem to notice it was a hospital. An hour later, someone showed up at my ICU bed with a stack of papers for me to sign.

Later, my realtor heard the whole story. He asked me, "Wait, when we talked on the phone, had you already crashed?"

"Yeah," I said. "I was already in the ICU."

"And you didn't want to postpone the closing?"

"Monday was the date, and I'm not losing this house."

He still tells people that story.

The Shift

Something changes when you almost die. You don't go back to being exactly who you were before. The experience cracks you open and forces you to look at things differently.

Before the crash, I was very good at being self-focused. Fighter pilots have to be that way to some degree. You need a near-delusional level of self-confidence to climb into a single-seat jet and fly into combat. You have to believe, deeply and completely, that you are going to win. That you are the best. That the other guy doesn't stand a chance.

That mentality served me well in the military, but it doesn't translate perfectly to civilian life. It can make you selfish and blind to other people's needs. It can make you think everything is about you, your success, and your goals.

The crash forced me to ask harder questions. Why did I survive when I shouldn't have? What am I supposed to do with this second chance? Is there more to life than just winning?

Shortly after I got out of the hospital, I read Rick Warren's book, *The Purpose Driven Life*. I started thinking seriously about how to use my skills to serve others rather than just advance my own career.

This all happened right before I started Ankerstar Wealth. The timing matters. I didn't start this company to only make money. I started it because I believed I could genuinely help people. I believed my experience and knowledge could make a real difference in their lives. The crash gave me the perspective to see that clearly.

Stewardship

I (Mike) came to a similar place through a different path. For me, it wasn't a near-death experience; it was a slow awakening that started in my early thirties.

I mentioned earlier that I became a Christian during that time. What I didn't fully explain was how completely it changed the way I think about money.

Before my faith, I saw money as a scorecard. The goal was to make the number as big as possible. More money meant more success. More success meant more happiness. That was the formula, and I followed it relentlessly through my twenties.

But that formula has a problem. There's always someone with a bigger number. You save up $1 million, and the guy across the street has $2 million. You sell your business for $50 million, and you read about someone else selling theirs for $500 million. The comparison never ends, and the satisfaction remains elusive.

When I became a Christian, I learned a different way to think about it. The Bible talks a lot about stewardship. The idea is that everything we have ultimately belongs to God: our money, our time, our talents. We're not owners, we're managers. We're taking care of resources that God has entrusted to us.

Thinking this way changes everything. If I'm accumulating money for myself, then every dollar I give away is a dollar I lost. If I'm managing resources for a larger purpose, then every dollar has meaning beyond my own bank account.

I started asking different questions. Instead of "How can I make more?" I asked, "What am I supposed to do with what I have?" Instead of "How do I compare to others?" I asked, "Am I being faithful with what's been given to me?"

Here's another way to think about it. Every dollar you have represents stored time. You traded hours of your life to earn that money. When you save it, you're storing that time for later. When you spend it, you're exchanging your stored time for something else. When you invest wisely, you're multiplying your time, so you have more to use in the future.

That's why I take our clients' money so seriously. I'm not just managing numbers on a screen. I'm managing their stored time, their life energy. The hours they spent working, sacrificing, and saving—that's sacred to me.

The Passing of Wealth

One of the most meaningful parts of our work is helping clients think about what happens to their wealth after they're gone.

I have many conversations with parents about their kids. Usually, the parents are doing well financially. They've built something substantial. But they're worried about the next generation. They ask questions like, "Will my kids know how to handle money?" "Will an inheritance help them or hurt them?" "How do I pass on wisdom, not just dollars?"

These conversations matter more than almost anything else we do, because getting this wrong can be devastating. We've all heard stories about lottery winners who end up broke within a few years, or trust fund kids who never develop any motivation because they've never had to work for anything. Money without wisdom is dangerous.

When a client wants to get their kids started with investing, I insist on meeting with the kids myself. The parent can be there if they want, but I need face-to-face time with the young person. I need to look them in the eye and explain what we're doing.

I usually start with the math. I'll pull up a spreadsheet and show the young person what happens when you start investing early. The numbers are almost unbelievable when laid out. A twenty-two year old who invests a few hundred dollars a month can end up with more money than someone who waits until forty and invests twice as much. Compound interest is that powerful.

But then I tell them something else. I say, "Someday, you could have a million-dollar portfolio. Maybe more. When that day comes, your parents and I probably won't be here anymore.

We'll be gone. But I want you to remember this moment. I want you to remember that your parents cared enough to sit down with you and get you started. There's a reason we're doing this."

That usually lands. You can see it in their faces. Suddenly, this isn't just about money; it's about family and legacy. It's about the love that a parent has for a child, expressed through practical action.

The parents notice too. I've had clients tell me they care more about their kid's small account than their own large one. That tells me we're doing something right.

The Tax Question

I (Steve) have a question I like to ask clients, especially the ones who are obsessed with minimizing their tax bill. I ask them, "What's your ideal tax bill?"

Almost everyone says the same thing: zero. They want to pay nothing. That sounds logical, right? Taxes are bad. Lower taxes are good. Zero taxes must be the best.

Then I flip it around. I ask them to ask me the same question.

"Steve, what's your ideal tax bill?"

"If I could pay $10 million in taxes this year," I tell them, "I would be thrilled."

They look at me like I've lost my mind.

"Think about what that would mean," I explain. "If I'm paying $10 million in taxes, that means I made probably thirty or $40 million this year. My life is going extremely well. Yes, I still want to minimize what I owe. I'm not going to write a bigger check than I have to. But my goal isn't zero taxes. My goal is massive success that happens to come with a tax bill."

Running a client through this thought process helps them reframe their entire perspective on taxes, so they can see that the goal is not zero taxes—it's making money. Some people are so afraid of taxes that they make bad investment decisions. They hold onto losing positions because they don't want to realize the loss. They stay in conservative investments because they don't like the tax hit from growth. They're so focused on avoiding the bill that they miss the opportunity.

If you really want a zero tax bill, here's how to get it: Quit your job. Turn off your Social Security. Give everything you own to charity. Congratulations, you now owe nothing. But that's not actually what anyone wants. What they want is success with tax efficiency. Those are two different things.

The Risk Conversation

Here's another conversation I have regularly. A client sits down across from me and says, "Steve, I'm very risk-averse. I don't want to lose money and want safe investments."

I nod. Then I ask, "Did you drive here today?"

They look confused. "Yes, of course."

"So you got into a metal box," I say, "and you hurtled down the highway at seventy miles per hour. You passed within a few feet of other metal boxes going the opposite direction. Any one of those drivers could have swerved into your lane, and you would have died instantly. You had no control over what they did. You just trusted that they wouldn't kill you."

They're quiet.

"Statistically," I continue, "driving is one of the most dangerous things you do. More dangerous than most investments by a long shot. But you do it every day without thinking about it. You accept the risk because you understand it and because the benefit is worth it."

The point isn't that driving is bad. The point is that "risk-averse" usually means "unfamiliar." People aren't actually afraid of risk. They're scared of risks that they don't understand. Once you understand an investment, once you know why you own it and what could go wrong, the fear usually fades. It becomes manageable and more acceptable.

That's why education matters so much. That's why we spend so much time explaining the thesis behind every position. We're not just managing money, we're managing fear. And the best way to manage fear is with knowledge.

Work and Life

I don't like the phrase "work-life balance." It implies that work and life are on opposite sides of a scale, and you have to take from one to give to the other. That framing causes unnecessary stress.

I prefer "work-life harmony." The idea is that different people have different situations, and what works for one person won't work for another. My situation is that my wife handles about 95 percent of everything outside my work. She runs our household. She manages our family's life. That frees me up to focus intensely on the 5 percent that's my responsibility. And the rest of my focus is on maximizing my clients' wealth.

That's my harmony. It doesn't work for everyone. But it works for us.

I (Mike) think about this differently. For me, the integration comes through purpose. When I know that my work matters, when I know that I'm genuinely helping people, the hours don't feel like a burden. They feel like a contribution. I'm not trading my life for a paycheck; I'm investing my life in something meaningful.

That's why we both keep doing this even though we don't have to. We've done well financially. We could retire now. But we don't want to, because this work matters to us. We're not just managing money, we're helping people secure their futures, teach their children, and live with less financial anxiety. That's worth getting up for every morning.

The Money Sheriff

Here's something nobody tells you when you become a financial advisor: You become the "money sheriff" for everyone you know.

Your family comes to you with questions. Your friends come to you with questions—people from church, from the neighborhood, from your kids' sports teams. Everyone knows you're "the money person," and they all want your opinion.

At first, this can feel like a burden. But over time, I've come to see it as a privilege. The knowledge we've built doesn't expire when we clock out. It stays with us forever. When my dad passed away recently, I was the one who knew how to handle the estate. How to file with the county. How to transfer the accounts. How to navigate all the bureaucracy that comes with death.

Those skills will never stop being useful. When we retire, we'll still be helping people. When we're old, we'll be the ones our neighbors call when they don't understand their statements. Our career isn't just a job; it's a permanent expertise that we'll carry for the rest of our lives.

That's what I mean when I say this is the greatest job in the world. It's not just about the money we make or the clients we serve. It's about becoming someone who can help, in ways big and small, for the rest of your life.

What This Means for You

You don't have to survive a plane crash to find purpose in your finances. You don't need a religious awakening to think about stewardship. You do have to ask yourself some questions.

What is your money actually for? If the answer is just "more money," you might want to dig deeper. Money is a tool, and tools are meant to be used for something.

What do you want to pass on to the next generation? Not just dollars, but wisdom. Not just accounts, but values. Have you had those conversations with your kids or grandkids? Have you shown them why this matters?

Are you so focused on avoiding risk that you're missing opportunities? Are you so focused on avoiding taxes that you're leaving growth on the table? Sometimes the thing you're running from isn't as scary as you think.

And finally, does your financial life have meaning beyond the numbers? Because if it doesn't, no amount of returns will ever feel like enough.

We started this book by talking about a client who discovered he was twice as wealthy as he thought. That's a great story. But wealth without purpose is just a number. The real goal isn't to have the most money. The real goal is to have enough money to live a life that matters.

That's what we're trying to help people build—not just portfolios, but futures; not just returns, but meaning.

Key Points

- Wealth without purpose isn't achievement—it's accumulation without direction.

- Every dollar you hold represents hours of your life—wasting it is wasting time you can't get back.

- Most people aren't risk-averse—they're understanding-averse.

- Stop and ask yourself: Am I treating money as a scorecard—or as a tool entrusted to me for a larger purpose?

Chapter 7:

The Emotional Side of Wealth

I (Mike) had a client who came to me after losing three-quarters of his retirement account. He had been day trading. Not occasionally, not as a hobby, but obsessively. Every morning, he would wake up, check the futures, and start making moves. He thought he could beat the market if he just watched it closely enough. He thought speed was his edge.

It wasn't.

By the time he found his way to Ankerstar Wealth, he was broken. Not financially—he still had money left—but psychologically, he was damaged in ways that would take years to heal. He had lost so much, so fast, that every small movement in the market triggered a panic response.

I brought him on as a client. I thought I could help him. I put him in one of our models—something steady, something designed for long-term growth with managed volatility. I explained the thesis behind each position. I walked him through how we think about risk. He nodded along. He said he understood.

Then the market dipped two percent.

My phone rang. It was my client.

"Mike, my account is down. What's happening? Should we get out?"

I pulled up his account. Out of all my clients, he was down the least. The model had done exactly what it was supposed to do—it had cushioned the fall. But he was still calling me in a panic.

I told him that once. I said, "Just so you know, I look at my entire book of clients. Your account is down to the lowest percentage of anyone, but you're the one calling me."

He paused. Then he said, "I know. But I've lost so much already."

That's when I understood. The day trading hadn't just cost him money. It had cost him the ability to see clearly. Every drop, no matter how small, felt like the beginning of another catastrophe. His past losses had distorted his present perception.

I tried to help him. I really did. But I couldn't get the day trading out of him. Eventually, the relationship didn't work out. Some wounds are too deep for an advisor to heal. Some people need to find their peace somewhere else before they can invest with any clarity at all.

Dead on the Inside

I (Steve) approach the emotional side of investing differently than Mike does. I joke sometimes that I'm a better investor because I'm dead on the inside. That's not entirely true, but there's a kernel of honesty in it.

I'm not devoid of empathy. When clients are struggling, I feel it. When markets crash and people are scared, I understand why. But I can see through the emotion to the analytics underneath. I can separate what I'm feeling from what I'm seeing in the data. This ability to see through the emotion comes from intensive military training and combat experience.

Mike is different. He feels what clients feel. When someone comes to him scared, he doesn't just understand their fear intellectually—he experiences a version of it himself. That makes him incredibly good at building relationships. Clients trust him because they know he genuinely cares. He's not just managing their money; he's walking alongside them emotionally.

This is why we make a good team. I'll watch Mike struggle with a client who's clearly not the best fit for us—someone who calls after every trade, second-guesses every decision, and treats every market fluctuation like a personal attack. Mike will keep trying to help. He'll invest hours into psychological counseling that he's not getting paid for. He'll bend over backward trying to save the relationship.

I'll pull him aside and say, "Bless your heart, Mike. But this is not an ideal client. He's got demons he needs to work out on his own. The experience that saves him isn't going to happen here. It'll be elsewhere."

That's not cold. It's honest. Some people aren't ready to invest with clarity, and no amount of hand-holding will change that. Recognizing when to let go is part of the job.

Here's the balance we've found: Relationship emotions need to be on point. You have to acknowledge where clients are coming from, understand their scars, and meet them where they are. Everyone arrives on a different path, with different experiences, different fears, and different hopes. That's the human side, and it matters deeply.

The analytical side is different. When you make investment decisions, you have to separate emotion from the numbers. You have to ask what the data says, not what your gut feels. As a pilot, when you enter bad weather, you have to trust your instruments, not what your body and mind tell you. When you listen to them instead of your instruments, you crash. Likewise, you have to look at the thesis and ask whether it's still valid, regardless of whether the recent price movement made you happy or scared.

Most investors can't do both. They either ignore the emotional side entirely, which makes them terrible at relationships, or they let emotions drive every decision, which makes them terrible at investing. The goal is to honor both—to be fully human in how you relate to people, and fully analytical in how you make decisions.

The Casino Mentality

Here's a pattern I see all the time. Someone takes $100 to a casino. They get lucky and win $1000. Now they have $1,100 total. Then they lose $50. They cash out their chips and walk away saying they're "down fifty."

How can you be down fifty? You walked in with a hundred and walked out with over a thousand. By any rational measure, you had a fantastic night. But that's not how they see it. In their mind, they had $1,100, and now they have less. The peak became the reference point, and everything after that feels like a loss.

This same mentality destroys investors.

I had a client call me recently about Palantir. The stock had pulled back about eight percent over the previous week, which is completely normal volatility for a growth stock. He was panicking.

"Steve, I'm getting killed by Palantir," he said. "It's down big. I'm losing all kinds of money."

My first reaction was confusion. I thought, there's not a person I know who's actually down in Palantir. We've been in that position for years. It's up hundreds of percent from where we bought it. How can anyone be "getting killed"?

I knew what was happening. He wasn't thinking about the 400 percent gain we'd captured on the way up. He was thinking about the 8 percent drop in the last week. The recent high had become his mental reference point, and everything since then felt like a loss.

So I pulled up his account and scrolled out to the three-year view. "I don't see this as bad as you do," I said. "Look at where we started. Look at where we are now. Yes, it's down from the peak. But the thesis hasn't changed. The company is still doing exactly what we thought it would do."

It took a while to talk him down. When someone's in that mental state—when they're anchored to the peak and can only see the decline—it takes real effort to shift their perspective. You're not just correcting their math; you're rewiring their perspective.

Mike has a phrase for this: "Your net worth is always the highest it's ever been for a minute, and everything is measured off that moment." That's exactly right. People don't remember the climb. They only remember the fall from the top. In their minds, they've never been up. They've only set new highs and then dropped from them.

This is why thesis matters so much. When you have a clear reason for owning something, you can evaluate it based on whether that reason is still valid—not based on what the stock did yesterday. The question isn't "What's the price today?" The question is "Has anything changed about why we own this?"

Covering the Chart with Paper

I (Steve) have a trick I use when clients get fixated on recent price movements. I'll literally take a piece of paper and cover the historical portion of the chart. Just block it out so they can't see it anymore.

"Let's start the conversation from where we are," I'll say. "Not where we've been. Today. Right now. Looking forward."

Then I'll ask them about the thesis. Take Palantir again. I'll say, "Do you think we're going to use AI and predictive analytics within the government to target terrorism?" They'll say, "Yes, of course, there's no doubt about that." Then I'll ask, "Do you think large corporations are going to use data platforms to make better decisions?" They respond, "Yes, obviously." Finally I'll ask. "Do you think Palantir is well-positioned to capture that growth?" They say, "Yes."

"Okay," I'll say. "Then stop looking backward."

The example above is what psychologists call recency bias—the tendency to weigh recent events more heavily than they deserve. If a stock dropped yesterday, it feels like it's going to keep dropping. If it went up yesterday, it feels like it's going to keep going up. The recent past creates an emotional momentum that distorts how we see the future.

Having an investment thesis is the antidote to recency bias. It forces you to think forward. It asks what's actually happening in the world, what problems are being solved, and what opportunities are emerging. It doesn't care what the stock did last week. It only cares whether the underlying logic still holds.

I've found that physically covering the chart helps people make this mental shift. When they can't see the history, they stop anchoring to it. They start thinking about fundamentals instead of fluctuations. They start asking the right questions.

Of course, history matters for some purposes. You want to understand how a company has performed, how management has executed, and how the stock has responded to various conditions. But when you're deciding about whether to hold or sell, the only relevant question is forward-looking. The past is done. You can't invest in yesterday.

The Anxiety Behind Responsibility

Over the years, there's something I've noticed. Many people don't want to pick their own investments, because they don't want to bear the responsibility.

If they pick a stock and it goes down, they wear it. It affects their emotions. They feel stupid. They feel guilty. They feel like they should have known better. The emotional weight of being wrong is more than they can handle.

But if they pay someone else to make the decisions, they're off the hook. If the investment goes down, it's not their fault. They hired a professional. They did what they were supposed to do. The responsibility belongs to someone else.

I don't say this to be critical. I understand the impulse completely. Investing is stressful. The stakes are high. You're dealing with your future, your family's security, and decades of hard work compressed into numbers on a screen. Who wouldn't want to hand that off to someone else?

I (Mike) see this play out in a specific way with clients who come to me after making their own mistakes. They've got positions that are down ninety percent or more. They're sitting on their statements like open wounds—constant reminders of bad decisions. But they can't bring themselves to sell because selling would mean admitting they were wrong. It would make the loss real.

So I tell them, "Let me clean this up for you. I can't fix the past—that money is already gone. But I can sell those positions and get you invested properly going forward. Just trust me. We'll get you pointed in the right direction."

There's something powerful about having someone else pull the trigger. It clears the conscience. It closes the chapter. My clients don't have to carry the weight of that decision themselves. They just have to say yes and let me do my job.

That's part of what we offer as advisors. Not just investment selection, but emotional unburdening as well. We take on the responsibility so clients don't have to carry it alone. When they're sweating over a market move, they can rest a little easier knowing someone is watching out for them.

Headlines and Manufactured Panic

If we went twenty-four hours with no news—literally nothing happened anywhere in the world—we would still have fifty channels covering it around the clock. They'd find something to talk about. They'd manufacture urgency out of thin air. That's what the news business requires.

The same is true for financial media. There's always a crisis. There's always a warning. There's always some expert predicting doom or promising the next big thing. The machine never stops. Every hour of every day, someone has to be creating new content.

I've been on the other side of this. I've done interviews where we talked for twenty minutes about nuanced topics—careful analysis, balanced perspective, honest uncertainty. Then I'd see the clip they actually used. Out of everything I said, they pulled one sentence and spun it into something barely recognizable. That's clickbait. That's what gets people to watch.

I remember seeing a headline once: "Jamie Dimon Hates Bitcoin." It was everywhere. People were sharing it, arguing about it, using it to justify their positions. But when you actually looked at what he said, it wasn't that simple. The headline was designed to provoke, not to inform.

Nobody reads past the headline anymore. They see the notification pop up on their phone—ding ding ding—and they react. They don't click through. They don't read the article. They don't consider the context. They absorb the emotional charge of the headline and move on with their day, slightly more anxious than they were before.

This fear-based news cycle is why we tell clients to be careful about how much financial news they consume. It's not that staying informed is bad. It's that most financial media is not designed to inform you. It's intended to agitate you. It's designed to make you feel like you need to do something right now, because urgency drives engagement.

Having a clear thesis cuts through all of that. When you have a clear reason for owning something, you can evaluate headlines against your actual investment logic. A scary headline about the economy doesn't matter if it doesn't change your thesis. A breathless prediction about a stock doesn't matter if the underlying fundamentals haven't shifted. You can consume the news without being controlled by it.

Modern Portfolio Theory and the Myth of the Efficient Market

There's a theory in academic finance called Modern Portfolio Theory. It won a Nobel Prize. It's taught in every business school in the country. In my opinion, it's deeply flawed when applied to the real world.

Modern Portfolio Theory rests on something called the Efficient Market Hypothesis. The idea is that all available information about a company is immediately reflected in its stock price. As soon as new information emerges—an earnings report, a product launch, a change in leadership—the market instantly processes it and adjusts the price accordingly. Because of this, the theory says, there's no way to beat the market consistently. Everything is already priced in. There's no edge to be found.

If this were true, stock prices would only move when genuinely new information appeared. You'd see a stock sit at one price for days or weeks at a time, then jump to a new price when something changed, then sit there again until the next piece of news. The market would be calm, rational, and predictable.

But that's not what happens. Not even close.

In the real world, stock prices move all over the place. They bounce around constantly, even when nothing fundamental has changed. They overreact to headlines, underreact to substance, and sometimes move for no discernible reason at all. The market isn't a calm processor of information. It's a chaotic mess of human emotion, algorithmic trading, and herd behavior.

I like to say, "None of us is as dumb as all of us." Individually, investors can be smart, thoughtful, and analytical. But collectively, the market does stupid things all the time. It panics when it shouldn't. It gets euphoric when it shouldn't. It prices companies at absurd valuations in both directions. The "wisdom of crowds" is real in some contexts, but it breaks down regularly in financial markets.

This is why thesis and conviction matter. If the market were truly efficient, there would be no point in doing your own analysis. You'd buy an index fund and accept average returns. But because the market is emotional and often irrational, there are opportunities for investors who think clearly and act deliberately. When everyone is panicking, you can buy. When everyone is euphoric, you can be cautious. When the crowd is zigging, you can zag.

The academics who developed Modern Portfolio Theory were brilliant, but they were working with models, not markets. Models assume rationality. Markets don't have that luxury.

They're made up of real people with real fears, real greed, and real blind spots.

So when someone tells you that you can't beat the market, that everything is already priced in, that you should accept what the crowd has decided, be skeptical. The crowd is wrong more often than the theory suggests. Big Box financial firms have been marketing this idea since the 1980s: "Beating the market is impossible, so trust us and put your money in index funds. It's a convenient message for them."

They profit when you stop thinking and start passively handing over assets. The underlying attitude is clear, even if they'd never say it out loud: We're smart, you're dumb, so let us handle it. Here's what they won't tell you, if you have a clear thesis and strong conviction, you can spot the moments when fear or greed has pushed prices out of line with what something is actually worth. That's where the real opportunity lives.

Confidence in the Relationship

I (Mike) don't think investing is primarily about confidence in the system. It's about confidence in the relationship.

When a prospective client sits down with me, my goal isn't to explain every detail of how markets work. If they needed to understand the entire system before they could invest, they wouldn't need me. They could just cut me out and do it themselves. My goal is to build trust. I want them to feel confident that I understand their situation, that I have their best interests at heart, and that I'll be there when things get hard.

I (Steve) think about this the same way I think about parenting. My wife and I have always had one litmus test for how we're doing as parents: When something happens in our kids' lives, do they think, "I can't call my parents," or, "I have to call my parents"?

If your kid gets into trouble and their first instinct is to hide it from you, that's a sign of an unhealthy relationship. Something went wrong along the way. But if their first instinct is to reach out because they know you'll help them navigate it, that's the relationship you want.

The same thing applies to clients. When something unexpected happens in their financial life, I want to be the first call they make. Not because I'm controlling or because I think they can't handle anything themselves, but because that's what a trusted advisor looks like.

I had a situation once where a client was at a car dealership. He was about to close on a purchase when the finance guy started pushing some complicated arrangement he didn't fully understand. Something felt off. So he stopped and said, "Hold on, I need to call my advisor."

He called me from the dealership. We talked through what they were proposing. I helped him see what made sense and what didn't. He made an informed decision. That's the relationship working the way it should.

On the other hand, I've had clients who didn't call. One guy got a significant inheritance. He talked a big game about investing it wisely. Next thing I know, I see a picture on Facebook—he's standing next to a Lamborghini in his driveway. All that inheritance money, gone in one impulsive purchase.

When I saw that, I knew the relationship wasn't where it needed to be. Somewhere along the line, I had failed to build the kind of trust where he'd call me before making a decision like that. That's on me as much as it's on him.

Building that trust takes time. It takes consistency. It takes being there when things are scary, not just when things are good. Once you have it, everything else becomes easier. The client relaxes. They stop second-guessing every move. They let you do your job. They call you when it matters most.

The Spouse Who Doesn't Know

I (Steve) had an old boss reach out to me a while back. He's a do-it-yourself investor—always has been. He reads the research, picks his own stocks, and manages his own portfolio. He is convinced he can do it better than any advisor, and honestly, he might be right. He's smart and disciplined and has been doing this for decades.

But he didn't call me to manage his money. He called me about his wife.

"She's ten years younger than me," he said. "And she doesn't know any of this stuff. Not a thing about investing. I've tried to teach her, but she's just not interested."

He paused. "I'm going to kick the bucket someday. And when I do, I'm going to hand off a significant chunk of money to her. She's not going to be equipped to handle it at all."

His solution wasn't to hire me for himself. It was to establish a relationship now—before anything happened—so that when the transition came, his wife would have someone she already knew and trusted. She'd have someone who understood their situation, who could step in and provide guidance when he was no longer there to provide it himself.

"I'd rather pay you too much up front," he said, "for the ultimate value of knowing you're taking care of my spouse at the end of all this."

That conversation stuck with me. Here's a man who doesn't need an advisor for himself. He's perfectly capable of managing his own investments. But he's thinking beyond himself. He's thinking about what happens after he's gone. He's thinking about the person he loves most and whether she'll be okay.

I use that story now when I talk to high-net-worth clients. A lot of them are like my old boss—competent, capable, confident in their own abilities. They don't think they need help. Maybe they don't, for themselves. But what about their spouse? What about their kids? What about the transition that's inevitably coming?

The relationship isn't just about managing money. It's about providing continuity. It's about making sure that when the inevitable happens, the people left behind aren't starting from scratch with a stranger. They have someone who already knows the situation, already understands the goals, and is already invested in the outcome.

That's a different kind of value than stock selection. It's more important.

What This Means for You

The emotional side of wealth isn't a weakness to overcome. It's a reality to acknowledge and manage.

Every investor brings their history into their portfolio. Past losses create present fears. Past wins create present overconfidence. The experiences that shaped you financially don't disappear when you sign on with an advisor or develop a new strategy. They're still there, influencing how you see every decision.

The goal isn't to eliminate emotion. You're human. You're going to feel things. The goal is to build structures that prevent emotion from driving your decisions. That's what thesis and conviction provide. When you have a clear reason for owning something, you can evaluate it rationally even when your gut is screaming at you to panic. When you know what would make you sell, you can avoid selling for the wrong reasons.

The goal is also to find relationships that support you through the hard times. Whether that's an advisor you trust, a spouse who keeps you grounded, or a community of investors who think long-term, you need people who can help you see clearly when your own vision gets clouded.

The market will test you. Headlines will scare you. Your account will fluctuate. Positions you believe in will drop before they rise. None of that changes your thesis—unless it does. Learning to tell the difference between noise and signal is the work of a lifetime.

Here's what I know after all these years (both in investing and from my military training)—the investors who succeed aren't the ones who feel no fear. They're the ones who feel the fear and think clearly anyway. They're the ones who have systems for managing their emotions and relationships for staying accountable. They're the ones who know themselves well enough to recognize when they're being irrational.

That self-knowledge might be the most valuable investment you ever make.

Key Points

- Most investing mistakes aren't analytical failures—they're emotional ones.

- Watching markets constantly doesn't create control—it creates panic.

- Anchoring to the peak turns winning investments into perceived failures.

- Stop and ask yourself: If I were forced to stop checking my portfolio for six months, would my investing outcomes improve or worsen?

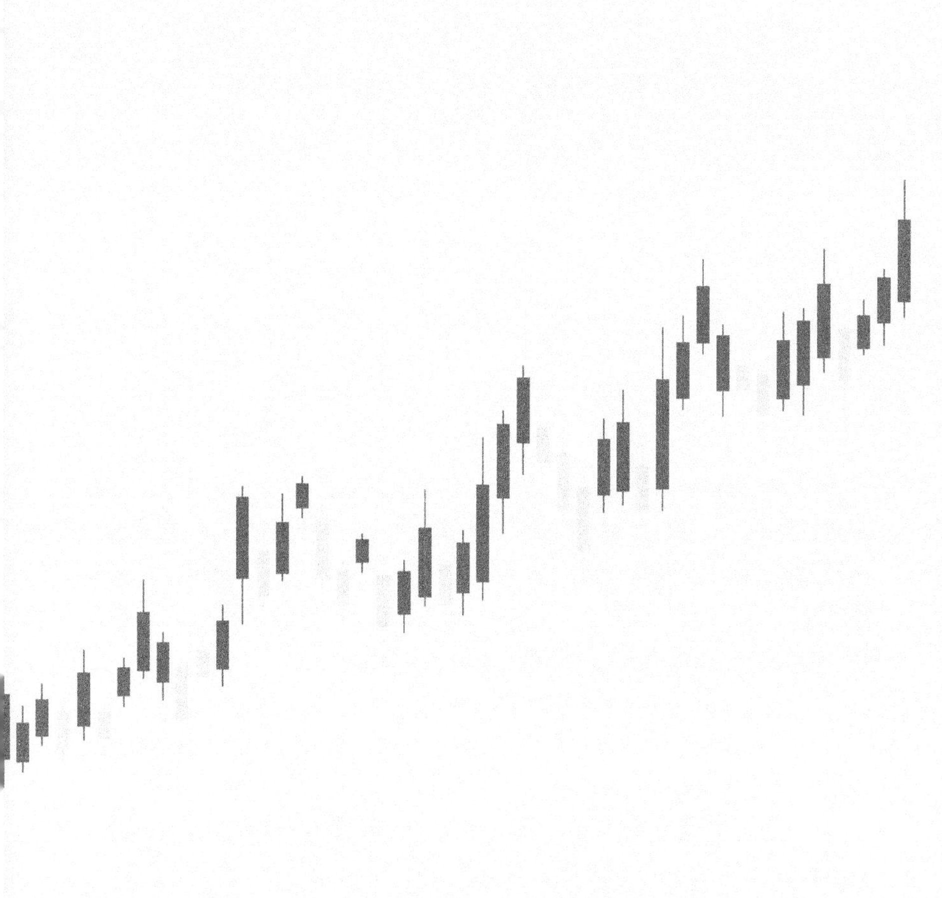

Chapter 8:

Maximizing Your Life

I (Mike) asked my father once when he was going to retire. He was in his seventies at the time, still working the farm every single day and up before dawn and out in the fields, coming home exhausted and satisfied. I figured at some point he'd want to slow down, enjoy some rest, maybe travel a little.

He looked at me like I'd asked something absurd.

"Never," he said. "I like working. Why would I ever retire?"

Then he told me about his uncle. This was a man who worked for the railroads his whole life. He had a good job, a solid pension. He did everything right by the traditional playbook—put in his years, built up his retirement account, counted down the days until he could finally stop working.

When the day came, he retired with a nice party and a gold watch. He went home, kicked back in his recliner, and started listening to Reds games on the radio. He was in great health.

Everyone expected him to enjoy a long, leisurely retirement.

He died a year later.

My dad shook his head when he told me that story. "He was fine right up until he retired. Then he just stopped."

That story has stayed with me ever since. There's something dangerous about stopping. Something happens when you remove purpose from a person's life. The body follows where the mind leads, and if the mind decides there's nothing left to do, the body starts to believe it.

My father is eighty-six now. He still works the farm every day. He's not doing it because he has to—he could hire people to do everything. He's doing it because the work gives him a reason to get up in the morning. It gives him structure, meaning, and a connection to something larger than himself.

When I think about my own future, I think about him. I don't want to retire in the traditional sense. I want to keep doing work that matters for as long as I'm able. That changes how I think about everything—including how I help clients think about their own relationship with work and wealth.

The Generals Who Die at Fifty-Two

I (Steve) saw something similar in the military. There's a type of officer—usually high-ranking and extremely accomplished— who becomes completely defined by their service. Their identity is the uniform and their purpose is the mission. Everything they are is wrapped up in being a soldier.

These men and women are incredible while they're serving. They're driven, focused, and willing to sacrifice everything for the cause. But sometimes, when they retire, something breaks.

I've seen generals die when they're fifty-two, right after leaving the military. They were in perfect health. They had decades of life ahead of them. But they couldn't survive the loss of purpose.

The problem is that military rank doesn't translate to civilian life. When you're a general, everyone knows what that means. You've achieved something rare and significant. People respect you, defer to you, and your opinion carries weight.

But when you move to a neighborhood in suburban America, nobody cares. They don't know the difference between a general and a private. To them, you're just another retired guy. "Oh, you were in the military?" "Where'd you go to basic training?" That's about as deep as the conversation goes.

For someone whose entire identity was built on being a respected military leader, that transition can be devastating. The purpose that drove them for thirty years is suddenly gone. The structure that organized their days has vanished. The respect they'd earned feels invisible. And without something new to fill that void, some of them fade away.

I think about this a lot when I consider my own career. One of the things I love about financial advising is that the skills never become obsolete. The knowledge I'm building now will be useful for the rest of my life. When I retire—if I ever do—I won't suddenly become irrelevant. I'll still understand markets. I'll still know how to read a statement. I'll still be able to help people navigate financial decisions.

That's different from a lot of careers. If you're the CEO of a ball-bearing company, once you exit, that expertise is largely gone. Nobody in your neighborhood needs to know about ball-bearing manufacturing. Everyone in your neighborhood has financial questions. Everyone is trying to figure out how to save for retirement, pass wealth to their kids, and make sense of their statements. Those conversations never stop being relevant.

Beyond Accumulation

I (Mike) have a problem with the American Dream—not all of it—just the part that says the goal of life is to make more, buy more, and accumulate more. That endless escalator of consumption that never actually gets you anywhere.

The problem is that there's always someone with more. You save $1 million, and the guy across the street has $2 million. You sell your business for $50 million, and you read about someone else selling theirs for $500 million. Elon Musk goes to the bathroom and makes $50 million. The comparison never ends.

I've watched people destroy themselves chasing that escalator. They sacrifice their health, their relationships, their peace of mind—all to hit a number that turns out to be meaningless the moment they hit it. There's always a bigger number, there's always someone ahead of you on the escalator.

I believe we have a much bigger purpose than accumulation. Money is a tool, not the goal. It's supposed to serve something larger than itself. When you lose sight of that, when the accumulation becomes the point, you end up with a lot of zeros in your account and a lot of emptiness in your life.

This is why we spend so much time talking to clients about purpose. We don't just ask them, "What do you want to own?" We ask, "What do you want to do? What do you want to become? Who do you want to help?" These questions matter more than the portfolio returns. The returns are just the fuel. The destination is something else entirely.

I've seen clients with modest wealth who live rich lives because they know what their money is for. I've seen others with enormous wealth who are miserable because they've never figured that out. The numbers don't determine the outcome; the purpose does.

The New Year's Prayer

I was at a party a few years ago—a joint company event at the end of December. It was a beautiful house, maybe sixty or seventy people—a very wealthy crowd. This was the kind of event where you look around and realize you're surrounded by significant success.

A few minutes before midnight, someone tapped me on the shoulder. "Hey Mike, can you pray us into the New Year?"

I was surprised. This wasn't a church event. These weren't people I knew from my faith community. They were business contacts, clients, and colleagues. And here they were, asking me to lead them in prayer.

I said yes, of course. As I stood there, watching the seconds tick down to midnight, I thought about how unusual this moment was. Here we were, at this wealthy event, in this incredible house, surrounded by all the trappings of financial success—and yet someone had thought to pause and acknowledge that there's something larger than all of it.

I prayed us into the New Year. It wasn't a long prayer or a dramatic one, just a few words of gratitude and hope and recognition that we're not ultimately in control. Then the clock struck twelve, everyone cheered, and the party continued.

I've thought about that moment a lot since then. It reminded me that even amid abundance, people hunger for meaning. They want to know that their success connects to something beyond the numbers. They want to feel like their wealth has a purpose larger than accumulation.

That's what I try to bring to my work. It's not preaching—I'm not trying to convert anyone—but an integration, a sense that faith and work and purpose can all fit together. It's not just about money. There's a reason we're doing this that goes deeper than the portfolio returns.

Steve introduces me sometimes as his number two, his CIO, the only guy better at math than him. What I really want to be is the guy who helps people see that their money can mean something. Wealth without purpose is just a number, but wealth with purpose can change lives—including their own.

What We Hope You Take Away

We could have ended this book with returns and performance. We could have given you the numbers and let you draw your own conclusions. A lot of investment books do that. They try to prove that their approach is the best approach by showing you charts, graphs, and historical data.

That would miss the point.

Wealth isn't the destination. It's the vehicle. It's what gets you somewhere—but where you're going matters more than how fast you arrive.

We've shown you a framework in these pages. Thesis and conviction is a way to think about investments that moves you from reaction to intention, from fear to understanding, from guessing to knowing. We've shown you how to ask better questions: What problem is this company solving? What would make this thesis wrong? How strongly do I believe, and am I sizing my position accordingly?

That framework matters. It will make you a better investor. But it only matters if it serves something larger.

You don't need to be an expert to invest wisely. You don't need to watch the market every day or understand every financial instrument. You need a clear thesis for why you own what you own. You need conviction that's proportional to your confidence. And you need the discipline to separate emotion from analysis, to ask whether your thesis has changed rather than whether the price has moved.

Beyond the framework, beyond the techniques, beyond everything we've taught you about markets and positions and risk—there's a question that matters more than all of it.

What is your money actually for?

And it's not, "What do you want to have?" What do you want to do? What do you want to become? Who do you want to help? What kind of life do you want to live, and how does your wealth support that vision?

Your answer to that question is where all of this begins to matter.

That's what we're really after. Not just portfolios, but futures. Not just returns, but meaning. Not just wealth, but lives that matter.

Mike's father is still working at eighty-six because work gives him purpose. I survived a plane crash and realized the second chance had to mean something. We keep showing up every day because this work lets us help people—not just with their investments, but with their futures, their families, their legacies.

That's the real return we're chasing. Now, we hope you understand why.

So here's our invitation. Take what you've learned. Apply the framework. Build your thesis. Develop your conviction. Become the kind of investor who thinks clearly and acts deliberately.

Don't stop there.

Ask yourself what your money is actually for. Ask yourself what kind of life you're building and whether your wealth is serving that vision. Ask yourself who you want to help and what you want to leave behind.

When you can answer those questions—when you know not just how to invest but why you're investing—that's when wealth stops being a number and starts being a life.

That's what we want for you. That's what we want for all our clients. That's why we wrote this book.

The journey starts with a simple question: What is your money actually for?

Your answer is where it all begins.

Key Points

- Stopping is dangerous—when purpose dies, people often follow.

- Accumulating money without deciding what it's for is just hoarding with better branding.

- The most successful people aren't chasing numbers—they're chasing usefulness.

- Stop and ask yourself: When others summarize your life, will they talk about what you owned—or who you helped?

Conclusion

Remember the client we mentioned at the beginning of this book—the one who discovered he was worth $8 million instead of $4 million?

He's still working eighty hours a week—not because he has to—because he wants to. The money gave him freedom. The purpose gave him meaning. And that combination is what we've been trying to help you find throughout these pages.

We started by showing you what's broken about the traditional approach: the cookie-cutter solutions, the fee stacking, the relationship desert that leaves you feeling like a number instead of a person. We showed you stories of clients who came to us confused, overwhelmed, and unsure whether anyone was actually looking out for them.

Then we gave you the framework: thesis and conviction. A thesis is your reason for owning something—explainable in thirty seconds, forward-looking, and specific enough that you know what would prove you wrong. Conviction is the courage to size your positions according to how strongly you believe. Together, they transform investing from reactive guessing into intentional action.

We showed you how to think forward instead of backward., how to ask what problems need solving, what industries are becoming more efficient, and what the next generation will need. We walked you through Bitcoin as a case study—not to convince you to buy it, but to show you how conviction develops over time through continuous learning and honest assessment.

We explained why we operate like a speedboat rather than a cruise liner, why we let winners run rather than automatically rebalance into losers, and why we meet weekly to debate ideas instead of waiting for quarterly committees to approve them.

Then we went deeper. We talked about purpose—the plane crash that changed everything, the stewardship awakening, the question of what your money is actually for. We addressed the emotional side of wealth: the scars that distort perception, the headlines that manufacture panic, the casino mentality that makes people feel like they're losing even when they're winning. We shared why we keep doing this work even though we don't have to, and what we've learned about the difference between wealth as a number and wealth as a life.

So what now?

Here's what we want you to do. Take the framework and apply it. The next time you look at your portfolio, ask yourself: Can I explain in thirty seconds why I own each position? Do I know what would make me sell? Is my conviction reflected in how I've sized things?

Then ask the bigger question: What is my money actually for?

If you can answer that—if you know not just how to invest but why you're investing—you're ahead of most people. You've moved from accumulation to intention, from fear to understanding, and from wealth as a scorecard to wealth as a tool for building a life that matters.

That's what we wanted to give you with this book. It's not just a strategy, it's a way of thinking offering not just returns, but meaning.

If you'd like help along the way, we'd love to hear from you. You can find us at AnkerstarWealth.com. Our door is always open for a conversation—no pressure, no pitch, just people talking about what matters most to you and whether we might be able to help.

Now go build something worth building.

Acknowledgments: A Mission Accomplished Together

No mission succeeds alone. This book is the product of a faithful team—family, colleagues, and comrades—who carried the load with us, stood watch when we were weary, and pressed forward when the path was hard.

To Our Families—Our Home Front

Steve's Acknowledgments

To my dearest wife, Irene, whose partnership has been the living embodiment of this book's thesis and conviction, applied to the beautiful chaos of our personal life. Just as a strong investment thesis demands careful research and adaptation to changing conditions, we have built our marriage on shared values and mutual trust, navigating life's uncertainties—from raising our family to weathering unexpected storms—with a conviction that has only grown deeper over the years. Your unwavering belief in us has turned everyday challenges into triumphs, proving that these principles are not just for portfolios but for forging a love that appreciates in value over time.

To my wonderful daughters, Allison and Alexa, who inspire me daily and to whom I pass the torch of thesis and conviction as guiding lights in your own journeys. In our family, we have seen how a clear thesis—rooted in purpose and planning—helps chart a course through school's demands, friendship's trials, and dream's pursuits, much like steering investments through market highs and lows. Hold fast to your convictions, my loves, for they will empower you to embrace risks wisely, recover from setbacks with grace, and build lives rich in fulfillment, just as you have enriched our lives together.

Mike's Acknowledgments

To my beloved spouse, Trisha—you are my steady ground, my trusted battle partner, and the quiet strength behind every step of this journey. You held the line at home with grace and courage, offered wisdom when I needed clarity, and spoke life into me when the mission felt heavy. Your patience, unwavering faith, and deep love carried me more than you know. This work may bear my name, but it stands on the foundation of your sacrifice, your belief in me, and your constant presence. I am forever grateful—and forever yours.

To my children—Spencer, Braxton, Nikita, Kya, Garrett, Jennifer, and Christina—you are my greatest honor and my deepest motivation. Thank you for your grace when I was busy, your humor when I needed lightness, and your understanding when the mission demanded focus. Each of you has shaped me, strengthened me, and reminded me what truly matters. You inspire me to lead with integrity, to fight for what is right, and to build something worthy of the legacy you will carry forward. I love you more than words can express, and everything I build, is build with you in mind.

To the Troops—Ankerstar Wealth

We are grateful for the entire Ankerstar Wealth team—our advisors, operations staff, and interns. You are a disciplined, principled, and mission-minded unit. Your professionalism, creativity, and commitment to serving clients with excellence make our work meaningful. This book reflects the culture you help build every day: intentional, innovative, courageous, and grounded in purpose.

Thank you to Candice Licht, Corey Hinkle, Jaden Verrico, Allison Ankerstar, Joel Hanson CFP®, David Chisum, Micky Barnard, Michael Majefski, Jack Peterson, and Alexa Ankerstar. Your talent, dedication, and heart make this mission possible.

To Our Book Launch Team—The Advance Unit

A special salute to our **Book Launch Team**. You were our advance unit—testing terrain, providing reconnaissance, amplifying the message, and helping us bring this mission across the finish line. Your time, energy, and belief in this project turned an idea into a movement. We are grateful for your service and partnership.

Allison Ankerstar, Joe and Deb Austin, Heidi and Scott Babbitt, John Bacon, Ann Berry, Rob Chambers, Ben Colman, Josh Curtis, Andrew Dawson, Maureen Daye, Alejandro Diaz, Russ Donaldson, Keith Eddleman, Lindsay Foreman, Claudia Gerard, Sean Gouge, Michael Gultz, Nick Guttman, Laura Halpern, Joel Hanson, Holly Harper, Richard Jackson, Kole Jimenez, Todd Johnson, Katrina Kidder, Kevin Lechner, Marty and Candice Licht, Christina Lleras, Jennifer Lleras, Pam Lintner, Michael Majefski, Stan Martz, Steve Math, TJ McLarty, Scott Nieburg, James Norris, Andy Papp, Alan Rogers, Ed Rosenberg, Gary Shelton, James Short, David Smith, Jeff Strommer, Jaden Verrico, Mark Verrico, Ray Wang, Jason White, Michelle Wolf, Trisha Younkman, Allen Green, and Janell Kelton

About the Authors

Steve Ankerstar is the Founder and CEO of Ankerstar Wealth, LLC, a Registered Investment Advisor with the Securities and Exchange Commission specializing in fee-only financial planning and wealth management. A retired U.S. Air Force officer and former stealth fighter pilot, Steve established the firm in 2013 (originally as Afterburner Financial) to address the need for affordable, professional investment strategies tailored to the upper-middle class. Under his leadership, Ankerstar Wealth rebranded in 2021 and now serves clients nationwide, emphasizing fiduciary duty, personalized strategies over products, and a keen focus on mitigating the impacts of taxes, fees, and limited diversification on long-term returns. Steve holds the CFP® designation and manages innovative portfolios like Bitcoin Alpha, Quantum Xtreme, and Xtreme Humanoid on the Autopilot app, blending high-conviction themes in digital assets, quantum computing, and humanoid robotics. His military background instills a disciplined approach to investing, rooted in rigorous thesis development and unwavering conviction—principles that form the core of this book. Steve is based in Leander, Texas, and is committed to helping clients maximize their lives through comprehensive financial guidance.

 **Mike Younkman** serves as Chief Investment Officer (CIO) at Ankerstar Wealth, LLC, where he leads portfolio management and develops the firm's high-conviction, thesis-driven investment strategies. He focuses on identifying transformative trends across technology and digital assets and translating them into specialized portfolios such as Crypto Xtreme Ex-Bitcoin, which captures the broader cryptocurrency ecosystem, and EGO-10, a concentrated portfolio of exponential-growth companies. His approach reflects Ankerstar's philosophy of evidence-based thesis building, disciplined execution, and resilient conviction in dynamic markets. Mike's investment perspective is shaped by a multidisciplinary background spanning healthcare, technology, and consulting, where he spent over two decades leading enterprise initiatives at the intersection of business and innovation. This experience allows him to evaluate investments through both an operational and strategic lens. At Ankerstar Wealth, he is committed to transparency, client education, and empowering investors with clear, actionable insight. Based in Lebanon, Ohio, Mike remains dedicated to advancing innovation and helping investors build long-term wealth with clarity and conviction.